THE LAST ALPHA MALE

THE LAST ALPHA MALE

THE AMOROUS PURSUITS AND HIGH LIFE OF A POOR LITTLE GREEK BOY

TAKI

For information, contact support@passage.press.

Hardcover ISBN: 978-1-959403-53-1
Limited casebound ISBN: 978-1-959403-57-9
eBook ISBN: 978-1-959403-58-6
Audiobook ISBN: 978-1-959403-59-3

Cover design by Wide Dog.

Library of Congress Control Number: 2025937261

Passage Publishing
Los Angeles, CA
www.passage.press

Printed in the United States of America

1 3 5 7 9 10 8 6 4 2

For my family, Alexandra, Mandolyna, and John-Taki

A special thank you to my daughter, Mandolyna,
and her efforts for this book, as well as her editorial ones for Takimag

There is no darkly burnished gleam hidden in my center, no nurtured secret of desire or ambition. I have tried pretty much everything I desired, and I can state with authority that the unlived life is one I know nothing about.

Unlike many writers of today, especially female, who desperately need to know where they belong in the universe, I knew from day one what I wished to be: Papa Hemingway.

—Taki

TABLE OF CONTENTS

ONE

What Is One to Do, Live Like a Monk?

NOT LONG ago, I was fast asleep late in the morning when I got an ear-splitting telephone call from Greece. It was from Vicki Woods, a *Telegraph* writer, and she sounded anxious. The conversation went as follows:

"Oh, hello, my name's Vicki Woods, we've met a couple of times . . . ah, at *The Spectator*."

Me: "Have we made love?"

Vicki: "Er—no! Ha-ha—absolutely not! But I'm ringing because—"

Me: "Why not?"

Vicki: "Well, I'm not your type, ha-ha, too old for you for one thing. Anyway, the reason I'm ringing is—"

Me: "How old are you?"

Vicki: "Er, forty-seven, but anyway, I'm ringing because—"

Me: "Forty-seven. My God! Forty-seven! Get off the phone at once."

So she did.

Yes, I know, it sounds terrible but at the time I thought it rather funny. Not so funny, as it turned out, for Vicki Woods, as she subsequently described in print: She was with her husband on the Greek island of Naxos, and they'd had a car accident. Her hubby was bleeding and there was no one around who spoke English. So she did the next best thing and called the only potential translator she knew, me, both a native Greek speaker and a fellow journalist. The trouble was that instead of immediately stating that this was an emergency and my help was needed, she'd acted like an Evelyn Waugh character—hello, oh, hello, hello, and so on.

And on my end, I'd assumed she was just another press hackette fishing for gossip, and so reverted to type, playing the part the hacks think I am—a conceited, arrogant womanizer who is always rude to women and the needy. When I read in her column what the call was actually about I felt like emigrating to Albania, though happily by then her hubby had recovered.

Not that I'm apologizing. Is it my fault I've been so often misunderstood over the years—not least by fellow journalists? Even the dimmest readers of *The Spectator* eventually figured out that not every word I wrote was to be taken literally, which reduced the cancel-my-subscription-because-of-that-fascist-pig-Taki letters to a trickle.

Although I'm nothing but an open book, it took an American journalist, of all creatures, and a female at that, to get me right. Taki, one Martha Sherrill observed in a *Washington Post* profile, is "nearly impossible to resist," he is a purveyor of "naughty quips and wickedness, sly compliments and flirtations . . . he is a rogue."

Moreover, "It takes about two minutes with Taki to realize that 'blindly chasing pretty girls,' as he puts it, has been his true life's work."

Precisely.

The problem, of course, is that our age is so weighted by the grim-faced insistence that political correctness must come before all else, with feminists leading the charge to turn most every pleasurable pastime into grounds for indictment.

How different are the jolly exemplars of self-indulgence—the Takis of this world—from these wicked creatures! With every puff that they do not take, with every seltzer water or arugula and spinach salad that they order, with every refusal to make a move on a girl for fear of showing "lack of respect," their constricted outlook becomes more the norm, the possibility increased that all pleasurable activity will be forever precluded. Long the rule in our universities, with their truly terrifying speech and harassment codes, such thinking increasingly dominates the culture at large.

I have always believed, and practiced, that lightness of spirit—humor!—is the best defense against the absurdity of the times. For it is jokes that take us where everyone of character must go—into forbidden territory.

My late *Spectator* colleague, Low Life columnist Jeffrey Bernard, knew this as well as anyone, and it made him an extremely funny man. He hated everything and everyone connected with the modern world. He was also an alcoholic whose column was sometimes described as one long suicide note, and having been married five times, women irked him something terrible. So he wrote an essay, based on an Alcoholics Anonymous questionnaire, in which he substituted the word "women" for "drinking." So it now read:

"Are women affecting your peace of mind?"

"Are women making your home life unhappy?"

"Do you show a marked moodiness since women?"

"Do you crave a woman at a definite time daily?"

"Do you require a woman the next morning?"

"Do you prefer a woman alone?"

The answer to all questions was yes, yes, yes, and again yes.

When it was published, a fearful imbroglio broke out. One extremely hirsute lady actually appeared at *The Spectator* offices threatening to burn the place down.

Now I realize that Mr. Bernard understood as much about women as Bill Clinton does about foreplay, but it was all in good fun.

Which is not to say that he didn't mean it, any more than to suggest that even at my worst, I'm not entirely in earnest. Where women are concerned, I am like Trump, to be taken seriously, if not always literally.

The serious part? As the hackette for the *Washington Post* observed, I am the ultimate romantic.

Indeed, I'll go even further. Love for me is not just a delight and an exquisite adventure, and the source of the greatest art and literature, it is the real business of life. Indeed, to win the favor of the fair sex is the very reason why men strive for greatness, not just in the glamorous professions of sport and show business, but in every realm of endeavor.

My entire philosophy of living has been built on this understanding, and among other things, it has enabled me to live my life joyously and without apology.

The great choreographer George Balanchine was a rare kindred spirit—rare, that is, in his willingness to acknowledge what most other men know to be true, but will not. When Jackie Kennedy asked why he was so obsessed with ballerinas, Balanchine replied simply: "Woman is the world, and man lives in it." For good measure, he added that while it is men who "take care of material things, women take care of the soul."

I will not attempt to say it any more clearly. Feminists can rant and rave forever, but every sentient soul knows that nature created the sexes as entirely different in form and purpose, and yet to be wonderfully complementary.

Ballerinas are merely a small part of my own portfolio. The fact is, over the decades I have been totally at the mercy of any attractive lady I happened to run into. No, actually it is worse than that. Incandescently porcelain skin in a woman can drive me close to madness. When a feminine beauty has crossed my path, invariably she has had the same effect on me that Beatrice had on Dante when first he beheld her. I've suffered a thousand deaths, fell madly in love, and gone to pieces until the object of my desire returned whatever I felt for her.

This did not come out of nowhere.

There are many reasons my father is my hero. He had a terrific Resistance record, first fighting in Albania as an officer in the machine gun corps; then afterward, during the Nazi occupation, having closed down his textile factories despite German threats, financing and publishing the chief Resistance underground newspaper. He was also the man who smuggled George Papandreou out of Athens and onto a waiting British submarine so he could head a Greek government-in-exile.

It was the specifics that were most impressive. No one had greater coolness under fire. I vividly recall the sight of my father's factories in flames. It was two days before Christmas, 1944. The Nazis had let them stand, unused, but with that enemy vanquished, the commies had now set them to the torch. Why? Dad was a capitalist, hence an "enemy of the people." He was upset but much too busy organizing the defense of our house to dwell on it. He had earlier acquired an anti-tank gun, a heavy machine gun, and plenty of ammo from an Italian officer in exchange for a suit; the Germans were rounding up Il Duce's soldiers, and the Italian hoped to pose as a civilian.

Already most of Greece was under communist control. Kolonaki, a ritzy residential quarter near the British embassy, was the only part of Athens still held by a small nationalist force, a brigade of British paratroopers, and the police. This is where the Taki house stood.

From the roof of our house, Dad showed us the flames of the factories. The fire brigade had not been allowed to intervene, and a couple of firemen had been murdered on the spot. Our night watchman, Fotis, father of three, had his throat cut by Red guerrillas when he went out to find bread. Our driver Costas was trapped but fought back with his Mauser pistol, saving the last bullet for himself.

The battle for Athens would rage a full two weeks before British reinforcements arrived from Italy.

All that day our house was under attack. I remember looking through the steel shutters and seeing a greasy-haired man in a raincoat with a carbine in his hand running toward our gate. He got hit just before he reached it, and his body lay there for days. We had one other defender on the roof—a policeman in his bright red beret, who later married our maid Lisa—plus old Dad. The house gave as good as it got, thanks to the Italian guns.

The funny thing was that we were never scared as long as Father was around. In fact it was quite exciting. Needless to say there was no Christmas tree that year, not much food, and lots of praying by my nanny and mother.

Late that night, Daddy slipped out of the house, to help in the defense of Makreyanni, a besieged police station under the Acropolis. Two mornings later, on Christmas day, I woke up early to discover a little toy castle next to my bed. Daddy had managed to cross the communist lines, find a toy store, and deliver it to me.

I kept that most precious of gifts throughout my young life.

And later in that bleak winter, when Athens was one great cemetery, he somehow foraged around and managed to get watches for my brother and me.

It is quite simple, really. For my father, honor was all. Entirely self-made, he'd left home at fourteen because of a dispute with my grandfather, and never looked back. I vividly recall his disapproving look at a six-year-old's fear when the constant Anglo-American bombing would terrify me to tears. Later, when during the civil war the Reds blew up his factories, he never once complained.

My father received the two highest decorations the Greek nation has to offer; one for bravery, the other for achievement. He never wore them, just as he never used the broken-down Venetian title his family was given long ago.

After the war, remaking himself as a ship owner—having convinced Harry Truman that since he'd lost his factories he was as entitled to buy American Liberty and Victory boats as the Greek ship owners who'd lost their vessels—he was the soul of generosity. As a businessman he created jobs, not junk bonds. He had hundreds of sailors on his ships, five thousand workers in the new textile plant he built in Sudan, hundreds more employed in his hotels. Later, he took care of my wife as if she were his daughter.

At the same time—and this I also admire—he was the most promiscuous man I have ever known. We're Greeks, and when Greeks see a woman the only thing that goes through their minds is to bed her down.

This has always been so. In the *Odyssey,* Homer has Odysseus describing a quick visit he and his men make to the city of Ismara.

"I sacked the town and killed the men," he says contentedly. "We took their wives and shared their riches evenly among us."

Just so.

In my father's view, it was a vice not to take chances, and he was the least prudent person I've ever known. He believed, as do I, that the truly great sin is to abstain from things that give us pleasure: eating red meat and drinking red wine, smoking, and chasing women. What else is one supposed to do, live like a monk, eating greens all day and never going on one's yacht?

The thing is to never be clumsy about it, or crude, and to always maintain perspective and a keen sense of honor. Although my father was one of the great all-time philanderers, he believed that duty means you never leave a wife, even as a proper sense of entitlement means you never unwillingly give up a mistress. He shared the same bed with my mother for fifty-six years and honored her to the last. And my mother, an extremely moral person, who never had a drink or a cigarette, remained steadfastly ignorant of his cheating.

Even his first approach to her was based on what Plato would call a noble lie. Upon meeting her, he invited her to walk with him in the Royal Gardens in Athens, where he claimed he had planted some roses.

"I should like my roses to see you," he told her. No wonder she fell for him. Romantics are assiduous flatterers, and flattery is only a euphemism for lying.

Yes, there are potentially disastrous lies—"Let me put it in, just a little bit" is arguably the second-most egregious after "the check is in the mail"—but as a general rule, truth is highly overrated, and never more so than in affairs of the heart. Needlessly volunteering information is self-absorption disguised as refreshing honesty. Candor is constantly misused as a whip or an affront. The fact is that reticence (and sometimes even downright lying) is essential if one wants to live graciously and kindly. One should never, ever demand to know the truth where sex and love are concerned. The surest way to hurt someone you love is to tell the whole truth and nothing but.

The excess of candor is why so many hearts are needlessly broken in America. In Europe, when a man tells a woman what went through his mind when he was with another, we call it cruelty. Only in America is it known as sincerity. And, of course, Americans also invariably pick the wrong time and place for their truth telling.

More, American "honesty" comes with rules and absurd prohibitions. For instance, in America, when I state that I find a friend's wife desirable, it is met with looks of incredulity, as if it is an expression of disloyalty. But I am the most loyal of friends. A wife's desirability has nothing to do with disloyalty or morality, let alone immorality. What would be immoral would be trying to seduce the lady in question while simultaneously trying to arouse in her doubts about her feelings toward her husband.

Quite simply, we human animals have our needs, emotional and physical, and the need for delicacy in our relations with others is the reason deviousness was invented. When properly used, words are a means of veiling one's truest thoughts. What kind of world would it be if at a party I informed a woman on first meeting that she was neither pretty nor well dressed? The sexes would get along even less well than they do now.

Life should be a series of successful poses. Parading one's emotions like a walking billboard leaves room for neither sensitivity nor imagination. It is the path to Armageddon.

It is, in short, Taki's view—as well as a core precept of my journalism—that there is no more innocent way of passing an evening than overeating, drinking to excess, filling up your lungs with smoke, betting more than you can afford on the queen of diamonds, and, of course, fornicating to excess. Far from being condemned, people who spend their lives in the pursuit of such innocent pleasures are to be cherished. They do not elevate themselves above others; nor do they try to oppress others and make life miserable for others. They are peacefully engaged in ruining their own lives.

TWO

The Making of a Hack

It was roughly fifty-five years ago, at the tail end of the Sixties, that I took the monumental decision to become a writer. It wasn't exactly an agonizing one. By then I'd been on the European tennis circuit for a decade, and was kaput.

When I'd first hit the circuit in 1956, it was a different game. An amateur game. Players had no chairs between games, no umbrellas to shield them from the fierce sun, no bathroom breaks, no injury time, no masseurs, no tiebreaks, and no ball boys to hand them a towel between points. The pros had not yet taken over and for the circuit there still remained, to quote the great book by Gordon Forbes, "a handful of summers."

I never lived up to expectations. I had good strokes, especially my backhand, and could run with the best of them. When I won the Sudan Open in 1959, the president of the Sudanese tennis association dared to predict I would win Wimbledon as he handed me the trophy. Shows what a crystal-ball genius he was. Never won a round.

I was absolutely no good as a match player. I used to get distracted, looking at the fans in the stands and dreaming about the consequences of a victory against an opponent with a beautiful girlfriend, if you get my gist.

I also had the dubious distinction of having drawn the second-longest suspension in the history of the circuit, for chronic bad behavior on the court, being outdone in the banishment stakes only by the American Earl Cochell, who'd knocked an umpire off his chair and used his microphone to tell the crowd to go fuck themselves. The great South African doubles specialist Frew McMillan used to call me Dirk, as in Bogarde, because of my theatrics on the court and he thought I looked a bit like the thespian. "Different sexual proclivities," I used to shout back at him.

The Fifties remain my favorite decade. Joining the circuit at nineteen, I hit the ground running, and traveled nonstop seeing the world. I was never tired or hungover no matter how much I partied—and I partied relentlessly.

And, needless to say, there were constant thump-thumps in the heart, as at every opportunity I pursued beautiful women.

I had a great advantage in this regard. As one of the worst players on the circuit, I was usually free to pursue the fairer sex by the second day of the tournament. To the losers go the spoils! Except in those days the females who followed tennis looked more like losers than the losers.

Still, there were legends of the sport to give one hope. Frank Shields Sr., grandfather of Brooke, was a renowned drinker and womanizer, and recalled as the best-looking man of his or any generation. He once followed a woman to Le Havre, where she boarded a transatlantic liner, and spent the night with her. In the morning he realized he was two hundred miles out and that there was no way for him to return to Paris in time to play the Davis Cup doubles against Borotra and Brugnon, and the Yanks had to forfeit the match. But he had not a moment's regret.

Nor, under similar circumstances, would have I.

It is said that romantic love, by its nature, is delusional and brief, a fine madness. I agree. It also thrives on danger, and it is this that excites me. Nothing is more vivid than the start of a love affair.

Needless to say, I did not realize when I made the fateful decision to emulate that other great swordsman, Hemingway, that a topspin backhand was child's play compared to scoring on an Underwood. As the great sportswriter Red Smith once described his struggle for a decent thousand words: "You sit down, take a clean piece of paper, put it through the typewriter, and when your fingers start to bleed you're probably getting there."

By the time I realized Mr. Smith had not overstated the case, it was too late. I had already announced to every jet-setter I knew that what the tennis-loving public had failed to appreciate was about to be recognized as a genius by thinking men all over the Greek—and English-speaking—world, and the Nobel Prize was simply a matter of time.

My father, for one, was not persuaded. When I was in my teens he had hoped against hope I'd go into politics. Having gone for sport instead, and unsuccessfully at that, he'd encouraged me to enter the business world. But now, instead of that, I'd chosen a profession one step above that of a whore.

This is how my brilliant career began. Some time before I had stayed for several days with Charlie Chaplin at his home in Switzerland. Although never a great fan of the Little Tramp, I found him absolutely charming, and he took a liking to me, too. We mainly talked politics, and, surprisingly, by that time Charles Spencer Chaplin had become conservative, so was particularly disgusted by the then-current student revolts against the allegedly totalitarian regimes of France and the United States.

I had taken some photos, and now, as a newly minted would-be journalist, I cut a deal with *Paris Match*—not unlike the one the Indians made with the Dutch over Manhattan. In return for full rights to the pictures, they paid me $400.

My father was so impressed with my business acumen that he forced me to promise to use only my Christian name in my new line of work forever after.

Right out of the box, I found writing easy. Well, it was not exactly writing; copying is the better word. But it did get me some instant attention. When an editor I knew asked me to write a story about the Paris polo season, I bought the *International Herald Tribune* and copied a racy type of reportage about the English polo season. Another hawkeyed editor spotted the fact that the only things that differed from the story that had appeared three days previously was the name of the city, the names of the players, and, of course, those of the horses. The instant attention came as a result of the editor circulating my copy around the room. It seems I had even left in some typographical errors, and my honesty made me a sort of legend for a while.

I beat a hasty retreat from Paris to London.

William F. Buckley finally took pity on me and hired me as an intrepid foreign correspondent for *National Review*. At the time *NR* was the numero uno right-wing magazine in the US of A, as opposed to the Republican party journal it later became (for there's a great difference), and Bill Buckley's writings were some of my favorite pickings. But his expectations were high, and English not being my first language, I thought the game was up for good.

That is when Bill's then twelve-year-old son came to the rescue.

Christopher Buckley admired my style. By this I mean he admired the girls I ran around with, my skiing, the drinks and cigarettes I offered him when his parents weren't around, as well as the tales I spun concerning the myriad Hollywood movie actresses who had fallen for my charm. In return for his admiration I asked very little. Only that after his parents had gone to bed, he would edit some of the copy I would be presenting to his father in the morning. Well, no, let's be more accurate. Christopher actually re-wrote everything. But he never changed the basic idea, nor my name.

This was an excellent arrangement, and was further enhanced by my marriage to my first wife, for whom Christo carried a torch. His ogling only encouraged his enthusiasm for my prose.

So writing was great fun that first winter I worked for Bill. But it didn't last long. When Christopher went off to school in New England I had to come clean to his dad, who actually used my unedited copy in lectures to students on how not to write. But Bill was a devout Christian, and felt sorry for me, so kept me on. He merely suggested that if I was not willing to return to school to master proper English usage, I at least try to learn by listening closely to the sound of good English.

Instead, what I did was sit by myself and practice. How does one practice? In my case, by writing love letters. I was smitten just then with an English girl who wouldn't give me the proverbial time of day and here, verbatim, is one of the letters I wrote: "Dear X. There is a marvelous line in *Romeo and Juliet*, when Romeo—having avenged Mercutio's death—is advised to flee Verona. 'But heaven's here, where Juliet lives,' he cries. However corny this may sound, this is exactly how I have felt toward you ever since the first moment I met you. Love, Taki."

Why have I kept a copy? Because the epistle served its purpose so spectacularly, I decided right there and then to try it again. Which I did three weeks later, when I met an American lady. I dropped off my R&J letter to her the next day, changing only her name and crediting Shakespeare because she was a Yank and otherwise would probably not know. Incredible as it may seem, it worked again. I was hooked for life.

Of course, it also helped even more that Bill and I had become close social friends, since we both spent the winter months in Gstaad, where he'd have me to literary lunches between ski runs with the likes of Alistair Horne, Dmitri Nabokov, Natacha Stewart, and movie star and memoirist par excellence David Niven. Bill would ring early in the morning and suggest a run somewhere, then he'd pick an inn in the vicinity where we'd meet David and Natacha, two non-skiers, and that was that. Buckley always referred to me as Führer, as I would zoom ahead first, followed by him and Alistair Horne, less steady on their skis, and at times near out of control.

Natacha wrote for *The New Yorker*—it was still a well-written weekly, not the race and transgender-obsessed leftie vehicle of today—and her main gripe was with having to put off attempts at editing. She would not permit so much as an iota of her material to be changed, and had the clout to make it stick. Which made poor me envy her as if she were Ava Gardner (an obsession of mine back then). My stuff was supposedly the second-most heavily edited copy in the magazine's storied history, behind only that of a German intellectual with a double-barreled name whose English was equally indecipherable when spoken. Alistair Horne offered the helpful suggestion that in lieu of journalism, I perhaps should try history.

"The Greek civil war, Taahki," he'd say, "you should try that."

But I pressed on, and gradually got the hang of it. Two wars in the Middle East and two trips to Vietnam for *NR* were brief interludes in my playboy life. But my real coming out was getting sent to Algeria to interview leading Black Panthers, including Eldridge Cleaver, who'd fled America after killing cops and was under house arrest. The killer quote from the homesick Cleaver: "Oh, man, what wouldn't I give for a hamburger and a black piece of ass!" *National Review* made it a cover story and I was on my way.

In 1977, I was invited to write a column for *The Spectator*, Britain's preeminent magazine for reportage and social commentary. Beginning a column for such a publication was like the first date with a girl you've had your eye on for a long time but never had the courage to ask out. It was a daunting prospect and a severe test of the nerves. *The Spectator*'s smallish audience was educated, sophisticated, and highly demanding, so it was almost like sending my weekly dispatches to an eccentric, unpredictable relation—one's Aunt Agatha, who graduated Oxford at age sixteen.

Still, landing the column could not have come at a better time. I had just met the woman I was to marry and have children with, those two events combining to turn me from an immature adolescent into some kind of man. Until I joined *The Spectator*, I had lived the most undisciplined of lives. Yes, I had made a modest name for myself competing for my country in sport, and had done some journalism, including as a foreign correspondent. But my true accomplishments were chasing women, spending time in nightclubs, and raising hell in a dinner jacket.

The weekly column and its demands anchored my life and went as far as to give me a purpose. Indeed, High Life, as it was called, became the center of my existence. The fear of old ghosts drove me toward an ironclad ritual of never missing a column. There'd be only one miss in the next forty-five years—not counting a ten week leave of absence as Her Majesty's guest in Pentonville Prison, following an unfortunate encounter involving white powder and an airport customs officer—the streak broken only when an assistant editor spiked a piece fearing I had libeled Jeffrey Epstein.

Speccie editors gave free rein to the columnists, and mine wandered anywhere I chose, from high society, to sport, to politics—American, British, Greek—and, of course, to the topic ever closest to my heart, the fairer sex. Culture back then did not yet put a premium on grievance, oppression, and victimhood, and when the libel writs followed in my wake Javert-like, *The Spectator* invariably showed spine.

My High Life column led to other goodies—American publications such as *Esquire* and *Vanity Fair* hired me, as did Rupert Murdoch's *Sunday Times* in London and the *New York Post* on the other side of the pond. "Write the way you do for *The Spectator*," said Rupert.

But those other places were never quite as comfortable a fit. The audiences were different. *Vanity Fair* and magazines like it appeal mostly to brain-dead dollies who don't know the difference between Rimbaud and Rambo, and they lack Speccie readers' well-developed sense of humor.

True, I also did a fair bit of undermining myself. *Vanity Fair* editor Tina Brown spiked my very first column in what was to become the magazine of the Eighties when I used it to review my own book. In retrospect, I suppose she wasn't wrong. I don't know why it is, but whenever faced with having to write for someone I've never written for before, I get the jitters—the same kind one gets just before getting into bed with someone very special. Self-conscious prose is like self-conscious lovemaking. No good.

Tina Brown later wrote about yours truly that "there are a lot of hacks who would like to be ship-owners, but there are no ship-owners who would like to be hacks."

It was the nicest thing she ever wrote about me, and for once she got it right. Even my father used to laugh about it, if a bit incredulously.

"Don't you realize that journalists make their living through blackmail?"

At *Esquire*, I very nearly got canned before I even started. I pulled a prank on the magazine's co-editors by launching a rumor via unsigned memo regarding their sexuality. Word passed down that the perpetrator would not only be fired, but he or she would also be sued. I was saved by a plump cutie-pie then doing a stint as a copy girl on her semester off from Yale, who was the only one who knew the identity of the guilty party. The cutie-pie was Jodie Foster, and she took her secret back with her to Hollywood.

In the end, five years was the limit I spent writing for any of those other publications.

But even at those places, I always tried to write with a free spirit and open heart, saying what I wanted to say, which I regard as the truth, and letting the chips fall wherever. It hardly needs saying that some of it aroused strong reactions, especially, and ever more so with the passing of the years, my attitude about relations between the sexes. For despite all the noise to the contrary, I regard it as beyond dispute that men are not by nature monogamous, and that the romantic feelings that launch them into marriage tend to be less durable than a secondhand Mercedes. Furthermore, I have taken it as my mission to publicly defend that most marginalized of contemporary species, the ardent womanizer.

I have accepted the inevitable slings and arrows and lived with the consequences.

True enough, when my *Esquire* column was terminated, I didn't take it particularly well. For a week I drank, and for the week after that, I chased after girls well below my usual standard. But then, facing matters head on, I accepted that this was the hack's life, sobered up, and went back to my wife and children. And c'est tout.

THREE

The (Ever Horny) Romantic

IT ALL began for me in an outdoor theater in Kifisia, just north of Athens in, to be exact, 1945. I was nine years old and had just seen Betty Grable dancing on the screen in a brief costume. Although I was innocent of the facts of life, an erection inhibited me from going for ice cream at the break. Which I was, but not in the way she had it figured. For the next five years Betty's half-naked image gnawed away at my poor brain, probably causing frontal-lobe damage. Then I saw Ava Gardner in *The Barefoot Contessa* and I began to have social behavior problems because of her. Later, when I'd finally meet her while playing Davis Cup in Spain, I was such a wreck she thought I was brain damaged.

As the years and decades passed, Betty and Ava would be replaced by Juliette Binoche, Helen Hunt, Renée Zellweger, and Ashley Judd. But the disease persisted. In the past, doctors diagnosed patients purely by observing their physical symptoms; internal mental states were seen as irrelevant, feelings considered too subjective. But feelings are what it's all about. Even in recent years, when I expressed my feelings for Ashley Judd, they were dismissed by both the mother of my children and my daughter as the silly crush of an old man. But the physical manifestations are always real.

The first girl I ever kissed was named Marina. I was about twelve; she was even younger. For months I had had a crush on her but was too shy even to contemplate speaking to her. The familiar story.

One day a friend of hers told me that Marina liked me. I pretended that I knew it, and then nonchalantly told Marina that I could have tea with her that afternoon.

Well, that afternoon I made what I thought was a suave move to try and kiss her, but I missed her mouth and ended up somewhere closer to her ear. I got so embarrassed I accused her of being frigid, but we did end up having our tea and a bit of a cuddle.

The next time I saw her in the schoolyard she was talking to another boy, and I threw a tantrum. In fact, I attacked her and called her a whore. She burst out crying and so did the boy. Marina never spoke to me again. Worse, to this day I suspect she soon began kissing the other boy and, worse still, that I drove her to it.

Lesson learned: no dramas, ever, and certainly no displays of anguish. For there is nothing that will keep a member of the fair sex farther away than a sad countenance. It is the essence of unmanliness. Keep her laughing, show concern if you must, but never jealousy. When a female knows you're jealous, she moves in for the kill. Which is to say, she moves away.

By then, we were living in America, having moved to New York about a year before. It's hard to explain to someone today how dramatic the change was. Up to then, I had seen only war and devastation. Dead, stinking bodies in the city parks, bullet-scarred buildings, people starving on the sidewalks, too weak to die in the privacy of their hovels. Now I'd been whisked from home first-class on a TWA Boeing Stratocruiser where I had my own bed and fell madly in love with the stewardess. But I quickly forgot all about her upon seeing the sights: the Empire State Building, the Chrysler Building, Grand Central Station, Fifth and Madison avenues, high fashion on Park, money on Wall Street. This was no mere city but a romantic notion, a dream come true.

I am not sure it's possible to convey entirely what New York, the idea of New York, meant to us who came from the old continent. New York was like the black-and-white films where people rushed about in a hurry, time was money, newspaper editors talked fast out of the side of their mouths, barking out orders to hacks who wore hats and smoked.

Women were beautiful and played up to the men. Mothers were worried and fathers angry, priests and soldiers honorable, cops kind and hookers kindhearted. And everyone was always in love in New York.

From the beginning, it was my kind of town.

My father put me into Lawrenceville, in New Jersey, a top American boarding school close by to Princeton. I was ten. The very first day I was punished for breaking the rule that no new boy, "Rhinies" as we were called, was allowed to walk on the grass, but were to stick to the paths, except during exercise periods. The reason I broke the rule is that I didn't speak English, which back then even students from abroad were expected to understand. (In those halcyon days one had to adjust to Uncle Sam, not the other way around.) I learned to *speak de English* in one week—not good English, but good enough to pass to the next grade the following year.

But I didn't make it much further, expelled for insubordination. I spent a harrowing three days waiting for Father to come and get me. I had seen his temper before and was not looking forward to it. But when he heard the reason for my dismissal—defending the honor of Greece with my fists—he smiled with relief and said, "I thought you had done something unmanly."

Throughout the next thirty years he would complain constantly about my way of life, but continued to support me in style.

I was then accepted at Blair Academy, a strict wrestling factory prep school, on the promise I had shown at Lawrenceville as a grappler. Although under probation, I did okay, even becoming captain of sport and proctor of school. One of my teachers, who also coached American football, approached my father during a wrestling meet and asked him to help a young Pennsylvania coal miner's son by the name of Bob Novogratz who had applied to the school. The Novogratz family were straight out of *The Deer Hunter*, proud, patriotic Americans of Polish extraction. Although one doesn't mention such matters, it is now more than seventy years, and the helping hand my father gave has been outdone by Bob's achievements.

Bob Novogratz became one of my closest friends while in school, was a star football player, and was undefeated as a wrestler throughout his Blair years. Bob was a heavyweight, and I wrestled 141 pounds. I managed to get him into trouble once after a wrestling meet in New York, when I took him to a nightclub and a place of ill repute, but he helped me pass my final exams via cram tutoring in math. Bob went on to West Point, where he became an All-American in football—a very rare thing as West Pointers were expected to know how to read and write, unlike football players in other universities in America. He remained undefeated in college wrestling, then went on to serve in Vietnam, ending his military career as a general. When I was in Nam as a reporter I asked for him but he had already been sent back stateside. I never saw him after graduation until we all went back for a 50th reunion. Another schoolmate and close friend, Gerry

Wynn, also a great athlete, had been killed in Nam, in An Loc province, and I spoke about him at the reunion. Somewhere along the line Bob got married and raised a family while serving his country. He sent his boy Mike to Blair, where he excelled in the sports his father had. Mike then went to Wall Street and became a very rich man. When I heard about it I could not have been more proud—it's what America is all about. I was a good all-around athlete and a good wrestler, whereas Bob was a great athlete and a great wrestler. I turned a great fortune into a modest one, while Mike turned his good genes into a large fortune.

Mike Novogratz started a medal fund in 2009 to help wrestlers continue wrestling, as the sport has been in decline for years. Like other low-profile sports that are not state-assisted in America, wrestlers have to do with far less. Now at least they have the motivation to win medals from Mike's initiative, wrestling being probably the last true amateur sport in the world. And my father had in some small way started it all. I am not surprised. Everything he touched turned good.

At fifteen, I was still sadly short of experience with the fair sex. I'd started smoking while at Lawrenceville—Pall Mall's unfiltered in a large red packet—but had not yet experienced the postcoital cigarette one dreamt of from the movies. (Smoking was illegal, but so was masturbation, which we were told by the wrestling coach was far worse.) My only plausible shot was "racy Gracie," the fastest townie, a pretty little thing who once let me kiss her. But when I touched her breasts, she told me I was too young, and by the time I had full town privileges, she was gone. And that was that.

I had a particular fixation at the time with Barbara Stanwyck, and when I read that actor Robert Wagner had had a four-year-long affair with her, my first reaction was that of envy and more envy. They'd met on the set of *Titanic*, a very good movie far closer to actual events than the blockbuster of forty-five years later that cost ten times what the real ship had cost. Clifton Webb played Barbara's hubby, an inveterate womanizer, though even a schoolboy like me knew that Webb was as gay as they come and then some. I wondered what the hell Babs was doing with a man who liked men when Taki would have given two legs and an arm to bed her. She was not a classical beauty, far from it, but she had S appeal, street appeal, that drove randy young men nuts. Although American as apple pie, she had an air of mystery about her, plus a pair of gams to drive schoolboys to onanism for life. Stanwyck played "loose" women, which in the repressed morality of the times drove me even crazier with desire. For four long years RJ and Babs did beautiful music together, while I rotted away in school.

On the plus side, my personal drought was at last close to its end. Since during my years as a schoolboy my family summered on the Riviera, I crossed the Atlantic regularly during the holidays. Back then everyone traveled by ship, with only foreign correspondents, spies, and the Zuckerbergs of the time preferring to fly. So I'd leave New York some time in July and return the first week in September. Needless to say, there were more girls on board those sun liners—as they were called—than there are emotional self-serving speeches in Hollywood during awards season, and the most beautiful I'd ever met was a Texan by the name of Isla Cowan. She was blonde, tall, with a Scarlett Johansson body, a Texas accent, and the reputation of being one of the richest girls in the Lone Star State. I was fifteen to her sixteen, dark, short, poor, but as determined to conquer her as Santa Anna was to take the Alamo.

Oh, wait, I forgot, I was not so poor on that trip. Since my parents were already in Europe and were meeting me in Cannes, I was traveling on my own. Which meant I could sign for everything I drank, and for everything others drank, too.

I was seated at Captain Jacobsen's table for my meals, as were the Cowans, those good old days being elitist and the captain not having to eat with everyone who could afford a first-class ticket. I made it a point to offer the captain and the Cowans non-stop champagne, and my ploy worked. Everyone thought I was a millionaire who simply looked much younger than his years.

Of course it all ended in tears. Once we dropped anchor in Cannes and my father came on board to collect me, all hell broke loose. Upon seeing the bills I had signed he began to shout, and demanded to see the captain who had allowed it. Worse, he told Captain Jacobsen and the Cowans what a phony I was. I remember having my last supper at the captain's table next to my father, and seeing Isla looking at me in the manner in which I imagine my old friend Joan Collins contemplated the bloated faces of her exes across the courtroom. Another life lesson: Hell hath no fury like a beautiful woman taken for a ride.

So that one was a whiff.

But the summer was just beginning. It was a month later, on August 11, 1952, my fifteenth birthday, that a young lady of the Martinez bar in Cannes accepted a $20 bill so I could truthfully claim to be celibate no longer.

I should note that these kind of ladies would remain among my favorites for many years afterward, and they gave me an education far too few get when they're young; which is to say, the kind of education I think is imperative if a young man is to grow into a responsible older one where women are concerned.

Indeed, as a general rule, older women are the best teachers.

Robert Wagner was twenty-two and the divine Stanwyck was forty-seven when they began canoodling together, which seemed to me perfect. For even then I instinctively knew that young men need older women for sex as much as (I'd come to discover), older men need younger ones later on. It is nature's fit, a perfect combination that carries the eloquence of the unspoken.

I am of course aware that many young men will disagree. I had a conversation not long ago with a young couple in which the female, all of twenty-two, claimed with utter certitude that her boyfriend is one of the world's greatest lovers. Point taken, who was I to dispute her experience? On the other hand, as I pointed out, supposing I suddenly took up golf and played two holes in par—would that make me a scratch golfer or eligible for the Masters? Humbly I suggested to my young friends that thousands of holes of practice are necessary to become a truly great golfer.

In any case, my next shipboard experience more than made up for the last. It was September 1952, and as a novice non-virgin I was returning to America with my parents on the SS *Constitution*, a great liner, sister ship to the SS *Independence*. We boarded in Cannes with the next stop New York Harbor. On board was a famous Norwegian female shipowner known as Oilboat Olga. She and my father knew each other and we shared a table in the first-class dining room. Oilboat Olga was traveling with her daughter, a twenty-four-year-old blonde beauty who was obviously bored, and in her boredom took a shine to me. We ended up in the sack. Needless to say, I couldn't believe my luck. Though I realize I'm contradicting myself, Oilboat Olga's beautiful daughter, hardly a veteran herself, sure taught me an additional trick or two. That we overdid things cannot be denied. We only appeared for lunch and dinner and never once made it to the swimming pool or the various bars. A transatlantic record may even have been set—at fifteen anything is possible.

So long did I remain in my cabin that finally my mother had had enough and delicately mentioned the fact to Oilboat Olga.

My father, in the meantime, was making a play for Olga, so the atmosphere became strained, to say the least. The captain of the good ship was of good Norwegian stock, so my mother, a saint if ever there was one, next went to him, dropping hints that both her men were acting in an undignified manner. According to old Dad years later, the captain played dumb, and assured her that it was all innocent fun. Knowing my father, he most likely had promised a port captain's job to his confederate after his retirement.

In short, it was the greatest, most dizzying crossing of any ocean ever, and that includes those crossed by Magellan, Columbus, and even Vasco da Gama.

When I got back to Blair Academy and told my schoolmates about it they all laughed in my face and said that these things take place only in the movies.

But of course, their fathers, whomever they were, were not mine.

A couple of years later, my father was pursuing a lady who had just been married to a friend of his. We all went down to Palm Beach for the honeymoon, old Dad taking me along to act as a decoy. In order to keep me happy he got me a brand-new Thunderbird, the first model that Ford put out. Needless to say, I was ready to do anything for the cause. On New Year's Eve we went to the Everglades Club, and by midnight I was totally sloshed. Boredom had set in with a vengeance, for it is neither easy nor fun to be a teenage go-between among lustful adults. My then new best friend, Sean Flynn, son of Errol, had been given a motorcycle, and he thought my T-Bird was for old ladies. Once my parents went to bed, I challenged him to prove it. We silently rolled our machines out to the beautiful meadow behind the club and roared off into the night. Though I won on acceleration, he finally got the best of me, which was a blessing in disguise, as it turned out.

Early the next morning, I was rudely roused out of bed in the Breakers Hotel by my father, accompanied by two extremely stern-looking state troopers. They took me down to the police station, and I was charged with the destruction of private property, namely four greens of the Everglades golf club. Sean was also there, looking sheepish and contrite. The damage was estimated at $30,000, which in today's climate could be closer to $300,000. It was $29,990 more than Sean and I had between us. Needless to say, his mother, the actress Lili Damita, an old resident of Palm Beach, and my old man came to the rescue. The club was insured and after some extremely stern warnings we were allowed to go home. The fact that witnesses had testified that I was a follower, not the leader, helped. Sean was put on probation, and I was told to stay away for fifty years or so. But I was back two years later, and meanwhile Sean and I basked in the notoriety our idiotic prank had brought us. We would remain friends until his disappearance in the Cambodian jungle in 1970.

It hardly needs to be said that sexual ferment in a teenager is ever present and all-consuming. A normal fifteen-year-old is a walking boner. At that age, I'd see an ankle and my tennis game would instantly go down the tubes. Before an important meet, my wrestling coach used to look at me while addressing the team and say that I would need all my strength tomorrow, so stop thinking of girls and think about how to beat the opponent. As the opponents were boys, I could have sued him for encouraging homosexuality. (Not that that would get me anywhere in 2025. In fact, it could land me back in the pokey for hate speech.)

Still, the biological fact of perpetual horniness in the male adolescent is so much a given that even in a world gone mad, the prosecutions of older women for the "crime" of seducing teen boys stands out as a particularly glaring absurdity. There was, for instance, the case in London of a beautiful twenty-seven-year-old ballet teacher named Sarah Pirie, who was tried and convicted for "abducting a fifteen-year-old," who (unluckily for him, bragging rights being what they are) was unnamed. In my not-so-humble opinion, this was the cruelest decision since the Athenians sent down poor old Socrates for corrupting the young.

Supposedly the alleged victim, the teenager, was reluctant to testify. You can say that again. Why testify against your benefactor?

Reportedly, the unlawful sexual activity took place between March and June of the school year. Without knowing the details, I'll bet the farm that March through June are the teen's favorite months, and the cheap hotels where the illegality occurred are palaces in his imagination.

Quite simply, is there a greater gift a twenty-seven-year-old beauty can bestow on a fifteen-year-old boy than sex? It's like winning the lottery. Not the other way round, obviously. No, a girl has to be of age. But for a boy, the greatest rite of passage takes place between the sheets when an older woman takes him to bed. What I would have given at that age to stop self-service and get laid with a woman ten years older than myself!

Fortunately, while at boarding school, I was sometimes able to escape for a day or two to New York. More than ever, it was my town! Broadway tickets back then were two bucks in the gallery and nine bucks up front. Movie houses charged a dollar, and a burger and fries at P.J. Clarke's—the all-night, most popular pub in Manhattan—could be had for ninety cents. And then there was Times Square, playground to Holden Caulfield, and young Taki playing hooky from school. Times Square was paradise for every horny fifteen-year-old, and then some: peepshows and strip clubs, and hardcore gay places we never knew existed. I remember paying ten cents per dance at Danceteria, making a deal, and then waiting until dawn for the girl to come out. Sometimes she'd emerge with a brute who told me to get lost; other times she'd go along with it, but reluctantly, concerned about my age: "You don't look eighteen . . . ." Those were the seedy glory nights of Times Square, before the place was cleaned up and totally ruined.

Like the woman of your dreams who has lost her looks, you wonder now if it ever was as you remember it. And yet it must have been, because I lived it.

But even then, sex wasn't all of it. Because I was already what I would remain, a hopeless romantic. Always—and I think this is normal in the male of the species—the base instincts coexist in harmony with the sublime.

I remember well back in prep school being stuck in a study hall for recalcitrant boys when Mr. Barrett caught me with a book under the desk while an unsolved algebra problem stuck out like a sore thumb on top of it. "Let me see what dirty book you're hiding down there," said Barrett, an extremely good-looking man whose face had been disfigured by burns when his bomber caught fire on crash-landing back in England after a raid. I was reading *Tender Is the Night* and showed it to him.

Tender was and is my favorite book of all time. When fellow students would talk in late-night bull sessions about their future plans, I only had one—to go to the Riviera and live like Fitzgerald's Dick Diver. After that, it would be Paris, in search of Jake Barnes and Lady Brett. Screw banking and screw ship owning. That was for dullards and bores.

"Keep reading it," said the master, "and screw algebra."

FOUR

An Empty Life, but a Great Education

AFTER MY graduation from Blair, I went on to the University of Virginia, Thomas Jefferson's school, where the rituals of spring are ever present: the cherry blossoms and the magnolias, the pretty girls in their shorts on Fraternity Row, the famous serpentine walls and the imposing Rotunda. Designed by Jefferson, the campus is the most beautiful anywhere on earth. At "THE" university, as Virginia was and is referred to by those of us who think Robert E. Lee is the greatest American ever, there were no women students except a few ugly ones from Charlottesville, but happily there were three all-women colleges within fifty miles from which to drive to and fro.

I was nineteen, and still cherish memories of careless sunlit days in Charlottesville, lounging around the frat house drinking mint juleps and simultaneously writing love letters to three beguiling sultry Southern belles now in their eighties: Mary

Blair Scott, Ellen Hurst, and Bonnie Richardson. All three were beauties everyone was after, and all three were honor students and very, very smart.

But Mary Blair, who attended nearby Sweet Briar, was my most consuming passion.

The trouble was that our romantic expectations—mine shaped largely on foreign shores—did not quite mesh. On our much-longed-for first date, the proverbial you-know-what hit the fan. Just before curfew I put the moves on her in my Mercury convertible. I'd barely managed a kiss, before she recoiled with: "What are you, from Paris or something?"

Still, it was wonderfully innocent, and made her all the more appealing. And when May came, the magnolias went into bloom, ceiling fans went into overtime, pitchers of lemonade were spiked with gin, and Mary Blair finally came round. She put on her white crinoline dress, and after tennis we lay out on the grass whispering sweetly to each other.

Her fan had an ivory handle, her skin was the whitest I had come across, and a tiny black cross on her chest accentuated her luminosity, as did her Scotch-Irish, blue-black hair and eyes.

Until then, she had never been kissed, not really, at least not in the French way, as it was called back then.

For me that long-ago romance lies fixed in memory, the sounds and scents of those endless days as vivid as yesterday. The sultriness of the South. Mary Blair's sunny disposition. The pure poignancy of youthful love. All accentuated by prodigious amounts of gin. That's what I call living.

No wonder I never hit the books, and I don't regret it for a second.

Heat has young men thirsting for young women, and Southern heat is known to drive men crazy.

But, alas, it didn't last. Well brought-up Southern ladies were not used to these things. For a time I continued to follow this

Southern belle around like a dog, quoting Fitzgerald, but to no avail.

Still, that the honor system was observed so strictly by everyone on and off campus in its way had great appeal. It made it easy to be a young adult. There were no scams or hoaxes to look out for at UVA in the early Fifties, let alone phony accusations of sexual assault or inappropriate language. No one talked about identity or empowerment, and only freaks swore. There was, in short, no one looking to instantly take offense, as so many students are today. Wearing a coat and tie was not mandatory, but the only one in my class who did not was George Finn, excused by his peers on the honorable grounds that he had fought in Korea.

It's not that we considered our ways the only right ones, but that we did not insist that all others were wrong. We did not seek to impose a single standard, or become upset when others failed to recognize truths that we held to be self-evident.

So the honor code really did encourage honor. And we can only look back today with nostalgia and sorrow at its loss.

Indeed, more than fifty years later, the University of Virginia would be the site of one of the most memorable injustices of the nascent "woke" era, when a piece by a female journalist appeared on the cover of *Rolling Stone* alleging that a gang rape had been perpetrated by UVA's Phi Kappa Psi fraternity. The story, which generated great attention and sales, turned out to be patently untrue, and *Rolling Stone* had to repent later—but only after great damage had been done to the boys involved, and to the school itself. Par for the course in academia today, and journalism.

Once college was done, my future plans were, shall we say, open. My daddy, God rest his soul, who almost never got it wrong, put it to me straight. He told me that if I wanted to live the very good life without working for it, I either had to do what he told me and wait for his death, or be adopted by a communist official in a country behind the Iron Curtain.

I chose the former.

In her remark about Taki and Paris, the elusive Mary Blair had been off only in her timing. A month after graduation, I stepped off a lumbering DC-3 from Athens onto the tarmac at Orly Airport and into a love affair with the City of Light that has yet to end.

Postwar austerity had left Paris cold and gloomy, but by now things were changing, the French having tired of shaving women's hair as a punishment for horizontal collaboration with the conquering Germans. Things were going back to normal. As the Roaring Twenties had roared because of the Great War's privations, so the fabled Fabulous Fifties were a reaction to the horrors of the Second World War. People ached to let go and have a good time.

I was twenty, ranked in tennis, and after being locked up in school for half my lifetime, was ready to bust loose.

There were no ugly sights in Paris then. Even the buildings covered in grime were beautiful. The smells of the city were unforgettable.

Romance was in the air and I knew it would last and last.

In fact, it turned out to be one long party. There was tennis at Roland-Garros, polo at the Bagatelle with the de rigueur celebration into the night. And there was the Parisian lifestyle—the venerable tradition of cinq à sept, a couple of hours of illicit passion stolen with a married lady while her husband was doing likewise. I could not believe my luck.

Most important were the friends I made. People such as Porfirio Rubirosa.

It is not for nothing Rubi remains a figure of legend. A gentleman diplomat for his native Dominican Republic, he was also a racing driver, great polo player, tough boxer, and future best man at Taki's first wedding.

But of course he was known best for his way with the fairer sex.

He married three of the richest women in the world, Flor de Oro Trujillo, Doris Duke, and Barbara Hutton. His other two wives, the great actress Danielle Darrieux and Odile Rodin, he married for love. European pepper mills were named "Rubis," after a particular part of his anatomy.

Rubi loved to be around younger people, and he sort of adopted me. I moved into his grand seventeen-room country house in the chic suburb of Marnes-la-Coquette. It was the most ideal spot imaginable because it was in the countryside but only a fifteen minute drive from a Parisian nightclub.

We'd box every morning in the tiny ring he had built inside his mansion—and when I say tiny, one crossed the ring with one left jab. I soon joined his polo team, and we'd drive into Paris to work the ponies at the Bagatelle Club in the Bois de Boulogne, where we played every weekend.

We also dropped in on Madame Claude's famous brothel rather regularly, having first dispatched Rubi's then-wife Odile and whatever girl I was with to go shopping on their own.

After every polo match there would be a party at the club, and on special occasions the dawn would find us playing without helmets in black tie. No one was ever seriously hurt. The practice was stopped only after a drunken Argentinian galloped into the clubhouse wildly swinging his mallet against the furniture.

It was nonstop fun with a capital F. When the film *Goldfinger* appeared, our friend Gunter Sachs, the filmmaker third-husband of Brigitte Bardot, decided we should make a spoof. Rubirosa starred as James Bond, a Greek billionaire of our acquaintance played Goldfinger, and I was Oddjob. We filmed for three days in Saint-Tropez but then a storm blew away all our props. Rubirosa, during the famous fight scene between Bond and Oddjob, swung a rifle that hit my elbow at full force breaking my funny bone, and the yacht on which we were filming, the *Creole*, went aground. Then our director, Gunter, took off with one of my girlfriends, a Chanel model, and that spelled La Fin for our film. But I would not have missed a second of it.

Which is to say, even the debacles were memorable. There was another instance, following a friend's birthday party in Normandy, when a few of us decided to forget about our flight to London and went to the casino in Deauville. Unfortunately, while gambling, we mistook a beautiful blonde for a pro, and asked her to join us back at the hotel.

Confused by liquor, we misunderstood her outrage, thinking she was just trying to jack up the price. Alas, she turned out to be the wife of an important French industrialist gambling at the next table. "Les anglais sont pire que les boches," was the nicest thing hurled at us.

Above all, in those halcyon days, there were parties galore, chic creatures moved to the beat of the samba, the tango, the waltz, and the cha-cha-cha.

Rubi regularly gave parties at his home, inside a large drawing room that opened up onto a vast lawn that looked over miles of field. He would install a small orchestra of four or five or six that would play nonstop throughout the night. The host had a canny ability to raise a party mood to almost orgiastic levels, and he invited only young good-looking people with impeccable manners. Rubi's party for Frank Sinatra was especially memorable, Ol' Blue Eyes announcing that had he known such beautiful people existed in Paris he would have skipped Los Angeles, Las Vegas, and New York. To my mind, it outdid even the legendary Rochambeau dance, the famous gala thrown by my friend Gianni Agnelli, the owner of Fiat, at the Bois de Boulogne; as well as the splendid balls that Guy and Marie-Hélène de Rothschild gave in their chateau outside Paris.

It may have been an empty life, but it was a great education.

Nor was it confined to Paris alone—all of fashionable Europe was our playground, along with the social capitals of America. And as long as Daddy didn't complain, I could easily afford it.

I attended the great international party at the Palazzo Serra di Cassano in Naples, hosted by the Duke and Duchess Serra to commemorate the 1960 Olympics in Rome, where many of Europe's crowned and uncrowned heads of state were present. Unfortunately, I remember little as I got very drunk with Leopoldo Serra, the youngest in the family. We began to celebrate early, after breakfast, when the crown prince of Greece, Constantine, won a gold medal in yachting. Aristotle Onassis got so excited by the Greek victory that he ran into the showers fully-clothed and embraced a naked Constantine.

A superlative week in Rome followed. Suetonius would have loved it. The best-looking, most spiritual, most poetic, and most successful seducer of Rome, Prince Dado Ruspoli, opened up his palazzo and invited only very beautiful young women and men of his class. Never have I seen so many handsome creatures dancing the night away as I did in his candlelit Roman palace. No models, no actresses, no celebrities, no gossip columnists, no nouveau riche types—certainly no paparazzi.

New York represented a different kind of pleasure. Manhattan then had more piano bars than immigrants, and there was a romantic, sexual electricity in those small cabarets. Cocktail pianists in smoking jackets played their hearts out over the noise of drunks in long seamless medleys.

That was the best part of the day, or rather evening. You'd pick up your date after a hard day on the tennis court and head for a piano bar while her stomach was still empty. Once you were well oiled, you'd move on to a restaurant, followed by El Morocco. After that, holding on to each other for balance, you'd head for the Blue Angel, where the maître d' treated me like a celebrity, and we'd stay until dawn. Then, owing to youthful horniness, it was on to even better things.

It might sound like a dull life, but I wouldn't trade it for a Nobel Prize for Literature. People stayed up much later than they do now. Even after a 6 a.m. drink, there was always Lexington and 51st Street for breakfast. Bickford's served good but cheap all-night food, and as there were no drugs back then, people actually ordered food when they were hungry.

The Little Club was owned by Billy Reed, a gay man who took a shine to me and gave me his best table despite my rather definite announcement the night we met that table or no table there would be no hanky-panky. It was at the Little Club that one night in 1956 the baseball great—greatest ever, as far as I'm concerned—Mickey Mantle tried to pick up my date Linda Christian, wife of Tyrone Power and the sexiest, naughtiest actress ever. A memorable night, indeed.

A bit of background. Eight years earlier, in 1948, an executive at my father's company took me to my first baseball game. I did not know the rules or speak English very well, but I was hooked—so much so that the old man blamed the executive when I began going around everywhere with a mitt, once even to a diplomatic reception for the Greek ambassador. And of course the Yankees were my team. In those days, sports heroes were genuine idols and role models. They did their duty, hustled, played hurt and underpaid, and taught the young the virtues of discipline and self-reliance.

In those years everyone loved baseball. Basketball was a game for freaks, and football was for college boys. Baseball was for those who loved apple pie and their mothers. I used to dream my father would buy one of New York's major league teams—at the time, they'd cost less than a tanker. Instead he bought a first division Greek football (soccer) team, and though I sat on the bench with the boys, it wasn't the same.

Anyway, that unforgettable evening Billy Reed came to our table and asked if I would like to join Mickey Mantle and Billy Martin for a drink. Is the Pope Catholic?

Even though it was obvious that Miss Christian's charms were what the boys were after, and I was clinging to her like a Siamese twin, my two heroes remained extremely polite. Though so dead drunk they were barely able to speak, they conducted themselves perfectly. It was a sterling example of what manners are all about. Anyone can have good manners when sober, even a rock star.

I of course did not begrudge my heroes' keen interest in my date—they were men, each with a pulse, and I might have been mildly offended had it been otherwise. But then a funny thing happened.

Appreciating my long-standing enthusiasm for the Yankees, Mickey took a liking to me, and forgetting about Linda (or at least pretending to), invited me to visit him and his teammates in the dugout. Mickey was an extremely good-looking All-American crew cut type, and I admired how he played hurt throughout his career, never once using an excuse or taking himself out of a game. He played drunk and sober, with or without sleep, and he was, above all, a gent, a farmer's boy from Oklahoma with inherent good manners and respect for those less talented than himself.

But this was par for how it was in that bygone era, a paradise of riches that I was privileged to enjoy. I would call every moment unforgettable, though given the breadth and variety of those riches, that wouldn't be entirely accurate.

Let's put it this way. Many years later, staggering out of the Waverly Inn, Graydon Carter's ode to yesteryear, I was addressed by a very well-dressed old lady, so frail her chauffeur had to hold her up. "Are you Taki?"

"Yes."

"I met you a very long time ago, on the Riviera. You were with Tyrone Power's wife."

"Madam, that was a hell of a long time ago."

"Yes, it was, but I recognize you. I bet you have no idea who I am."

In fact, I did not, but I pretended to remember in order not to hurt the lady's feelings.

Only afterward did it hit me, and I wished it hadn't.

I had indeed been on the Riviera with Linda Christian. But fool that I was, I'd naughtily snuck out of our hotel to meet the lady in question at hers. Alas, while on the saddle, the lady's boyfriend walked in on us and attacked me with a vase and I was forced to make a rather hasty retreat in my birthday suit. By the time I returned to my love nest with Linda I was shaken and badly disheveled. And Linda, whose own behavior in the sack was matched by her tempestuousness elsewhere, was not pleased.

It was not my finest hour, but then I was all of nineteen at the time.

Still, there was nothing to do but take my lumps—and given the prize, I took them gladly.

Any man would have done that and more for Linda Christian.

Did the life have its drawbacks? None that I can think of. But risks and consequences, yes. The first woman whose husband I ever cuckolded was a French-born beauty and Greek shipowner's wife. He was forty-two and I was nineteen. We were immediately discovered and I was dispatched to Paris by my father once her husband had filed for divorce and named me as correspondent. One year later, back in New York, more problems. This time a society lady became pregnant and was demanding marriage. Back to Paris, all expenses paid. (The good news is she was pretending.) Over the years, I have gone on to cuckold my fair share of husbands, and am not aware I have ever been cuckolded in return. (Although the husband is usually the last to know.)

When I'm in Manhattan today, I still walk everywhere, and when I see rows of lovely townhouses and low-rise multifamily dwellings nostalgia hits like the proverbial gong: a snatched kiss with a married lady during Thanksgiving 1962, a song on the radio in a convertible outside a young girl's house with her roommates looking down at us.

But gosh—to usc an expression that's also out of date—how things have changed! Even then the end of elegance was already in sight, but it would hit New York, with its excess of vulgar new-rich social climbers and quasi-celebrities, more swiftly than anywhere else.

My liaison with Linda Christian began when she was thirty-three to my nineteen, and lasted two years. I then began one with another star, but she got rid of me pronto. A year after that, in 1957, I was smitten by the charms of a nice Jewish girl with blue eyes and a great pair of legs whose name was Joan Collins. That one was rather exhausting. I was living at the Beverly Hills Hotel, and when I was not with Miss C, I was fighting the many and various Hollywood types who wanted to take my place. The end was inevitable. When Nicky Hilton's turn came I knew my time was up, since at the time Hilton "owned" Hollywood, and any victory on my part was bound to be a Pyrrhic one. When we eventually came to blows, it was a draw, but I was left with two black eyes and his nose was rearranged for good. Plus, no one in Hollywood dared to speak to me after that. Worse, no gals would go out with me.

Right then and there I decided Hollywood women were as bad as Hollywood men, and I can't think of anything worse to say about anyone. No more actresses for me, I swore at the time, and although I did go back to that hellhole a couple more times, I never once went near a member of the fair sex who made her living in front of a camera.

Well, no, that's not quite true.

When I met Brigitte Bardot, she was at the height of her fame, the wet dream of every red-blooded man this side of

Baghdad, and France's most famous export. She was the original girl/woman, pouting, flirting, falling out of love on screen and off. It was 1968, just after she'd married my future director Gunter Sachs. That was a lousy year for the poor little Greek boy. My tennis career, if one could call it that, was coming to an end. Years of sleepless nights had taken their toll, and an already weak game was turning into an embarrassing one. I knew the circuit and I were through after a particularly embarrassing loss to a kid so young he could hardly reach over the net to shake hands after the match. Needless to say, my father was getting fed up with me.

So I went to Saint-Tropez—where else?—for some R&R and Brigitte invited me to stay at La Madrague, her fabled house on the outskirts of town.

It was quite a course in celebrity. For starters, we were about twenty live-in guests: a few close friends, a few hangers-on, some wannabe hangers-on, very few servants, plus her father and sister. The help ate with us and cleaned up afterward, though otherwise acted like privileged guests.

Mijanou Bardot was sexier than her older sister and had a nicer personality. Though BB and I were just friends, since most of her boys were gigolos, everyone thought I was her latest toy boy.

After a couple of weeks in La Madrague I flew to Greece, and as it happened BB had chartered a boat to cruise the isles. We'd made vague plans to meet.

When she landed in Athens, the colonels, who'd lately seized power, made sure the whole world knew about it, since she was among the first celebrities to visit the cradle of democracy after parliament had been done away with.

In a chaotic press conference she was asked the usual platitudes about my country and then whether she knew any Greeks. "Yes," she answered, "I know Taki Theodoracopulos."

"What is your relationship?"

"Je l'aime beaucoup," she said, using the French manner of expressing friendship.

But this was Greece, where victories are rare and where the press only occasionally inject facts into a story (it is still that way).

Thirty years later, when the Brit mag *Tatler* published spoof odds on who might one day marry Princess Diana, my chances were quoted at 11-1 and Constantine Niarchos's at 33-1, and a respected Greek newspaper headlined it as: "Two of Our Boys in the Top 10."

Needless to say, two hundred paparazzi were outside my humble home quicker than you can say moussaka, forcing me to disappear. "I need, I must, I have to see my love Taki, sobs Bardot," was one of the more responsible headlines.

It was the only time in her life my mother ever spoke to a hack. She addressed the motley ones assembled outside her house and declared that adultery was against the Ten Commandments, ergo Miss Bardot could not have her son.

My old Dad said nothing but tried to seduce her by anchoring near her somewhere in the Aegean.

In any event, the glorious, carefree days of my youth were about to come to an abrupt and terrible end.

The cause, of course, was a woman—or, more to the point, a foolish lovesick Taki.

The woman I was madly in love with spent my money quicker than Usain Bolt would one day run the 100, but she was beautiful, and teaching me rather a lot about sex, so what was I supposed to do, take her to the automat?

Rather than ask my father for further funds, expecting he would be appalled, I did what seemed the next logical thing—I went to a Mafia guy in New York and borrowed $2,000, signing a note agreeing that I would pay back $4,000 in one week's time. After all, I was young back then, a week was like ten years today. Anything could happen: nuclear war, a natural catastrophe, maybe an asteroid. So the lady and I flew to Paris and had a pretty good time spending the money, then I cut the holiday short by one day and like an absconding party-crasher flew to Athens when a sudden desire to see my parents overcame me. The first person I met as I came into my house was a New Yorker whose face looked familiar. I owed him 4,000 greenbacks.

Dad was very understanding. He knew what the Mafia do when they don't get what they want. He paid the Mafioso, going so far as to praise me in front of him for my business acumen. But then he decided it was time to teach me a lesson. He'd send me to work in one of his textile factories in the Sudan.

Worse, he dispatched me to Khartoum by tourist class. Worse still, the airplane was full and I was assigned the middle seat between two Arab gentlemen. I will not go further into the gory details of my martyrdom. Suffice it to say, never have I prayed more for an airplane to crash.

FIVE

Oh, for the *Grandes Horizontales* of Old

ACTUALLY, KHARTOUM turned out to be not such a bad place back then. I hung out and hit balls every morning with the great tennis player Gottfried von Cramm, who'd reached the final at Wimbledon three times and twice won the French championships, the slow clay being perfect for his beautiful flat strokes and devastating second spin serve. Now he cheered me on from the stands as I won the Sudan open.

Evenings were spent socializing with the likes of Alfried Krupp at the Gordon nightclub, and day and night—at least weeknights—I was in love with Grace, a great beauty of her time, and of that place. On weekends, I'd visit Egypt, where I played tennis at the Gezira Sporting Club, gambled at the Mohammed Ali Club, and was in love with a Levantine lady. Though this was six years after King Farouk's fall, life there was still very sweet.

In Khartoum I had a driver, Zacki, as well as a personal servant, Abdu, whereas before my punishment/banishment I'd had neither. So I did my time manfully.

See what I mean about youth? One doesn't give a damn, and never worries about tomorrow, and can adjust to anything. Faust was no fool.

My father had decided to build the Sundanese textile mega factory some years before, after reading in a newspaper that Sudan imported cloth despite being one of the world's great cotton producers—the coals to Newcastle syndrome. So off he went to Khartoum. He tapped the British Minister of Transport, Ernest Marples, to head the consortium to construct it, and in no time built the largest textile mill in the Middle East, with 3,000 looms and 55,000 spindles. It was called Sudan-American Textile Industry, as Washington had loaned him ten million big ones, and it was a showplace. Fully air-conditioned, its 5,000 workers toiled in comfort.

Sudan's president at the time was Ibrahim Abboud, my all-time favorite strongman. He was a popular and decent general who'd been invited to assume power in 1958. I visited him once a week to hand him an envelope from my father, and his only bad habit was picking his nose just before shaking my hand.

But Arab nationalism was in the air, fanned by Egypt's Nasser, and when our man Abboud was overthrown five years later, my father's factory was the first in the region to be nationalized. The 5,000 workers all lost their jobs, and within two years of the "Africa for the Africans" government of the Mahdi, the factory was burned to the ground.

Needless to say, Sudan has now gone even further to hell. Once the breadbasket of Africa, along with Zimbabwe, it is run by psychopathic murderers and has people starving in the streets, for which leftists blame the West. But of course these atrocities would not be happening to Zimbabwe and Sudan if they were still run by the Brits—but no such luck for those poor bastards.

But the subject at hand is how I redeemed myself, and got back in my father's good graces. This, in turn, brings me to the not unrelated topic of prostitution.

When Kipling made his famous quip about journalists having "power without responsibility," he needlessly added the phrase "the prerogative of the harlot throughout the ages."

Taki is here to tell you that comparing hacks to prostitutes could not be more unfair to the girls. Hookers are infinitely more trustworthy than hacks, and in every way more deserving of respect.

Nonetheless, working girls have been mistrusted and maligned as far back as the Bible.

During Britain's great Profumo affair of 1963, millions of Britons wondered how John Profumo, the distinguished Secretary of State for War, could possibly have betrayed his beautiful film-star wife Valerie Hobson for a winsome nineteen-year-old hooker, Christine Keeler. How little they know of life! As those in Taki's circle well know, the lovelier the wife, the more fun it is to cheat. Still, eventually Profumo was justly rehabilitated. Not so poor Christine. Blameless as she was, she ended up an outcast and broke.

Of course, distinctions must be made. There is prostitution and prostitution—and I'm speaking of the girls with a high-end clientele, not the many unfortunates now working in London, Paris, and Milan from Eastern Europe trafficked by pimps, whose clients are almost as grubby and even uglier than the pimps.

Where both kinds are sex workers, as they now like to call themselves, their existences are obviously of an entirely different order.

I once asked an American automobile tycoon—okay, it was Henry Ford II—whom from the past he would have liked to dine with à deux, and he immediately answered Paul Valéry. The

French poet? I was both surprised and impressed. "How come Paul-Valéry?" I asked. "Which poem?"

"Poem? What poem? It's my favorite whorehouse on rue Paul-Valéry in Paris."

Sure enough, he was right. Madame Billy's was a whorehouse in rue Paul-Valéry; I myself had once been a regular client. Back then, when classy girls didn't give it away as often as they do nowadays, whorehouses were good business.

But as every connoisseur knows, Billy was eventually eclipsed by Madame Claude, whose establishment on rue de Marignan was known affectionately as the Goody, Goody Gumdrops Room. Claude's was the plus ultra in quality of service well into the Sixties.

Madame Claude, France's greatest madame, was in fact Fernande Grudet, who came up from the streets. She was a nice woman who played fair with the girls, semi-pros at best, since brainy jobs being scarce for women back then, girls had to rely mostly on their looks. But some were real lookers. She never told me what percentage she took, but she tried to protect the girls by picking certain nice clients for particularly delicate gals.

When I was first in Paris, under the tutelage of Rubi, I regularly used Madame Claude's girls. (Never on Sunday, at least after I was first married, for I would always be with my wife after playing polo.) Although I say so myself, I was considered a nice John, clean, young, thin, mercifully quick, and very discreet when I'd occasionally meet them after action with their boyfriends chez Castel's or New Jimmy's.

Discretion was key, as much for the clients as for the girls themselves. Men who talk are worse than those with crabs, as Madame Claude herself once put it to me. Aside from all the rest, it was the quickest way to stop getting lucky.

I remember being once in a sauna with three very famous playboys. It was in the midst of Edmond de Rothschild's party in Megève, a blast that lasted three days and nights, and we were recovering and trying to sweat it out when a certain lady's name came up. She was a famous film star. We all looked at each other because all four of us had stepped out with her. No one said a word except for Jean Poniatowski, descendant of Napoleon's marshal who died during the retreat from Russia, because he was the only one who hadn't gotten lucky. "I've never met her," he lied. "What's she . . . like?"

"Leave the sauna at once," said Gianni Agnelli—his light-hearted way of pointing out the faux pas.

In short, we tolerated none of the tell-me-the-details crap of today.

Not only didn't men I grew up with do such things, neither did the women.

Neither did Madame Claude. She eventually ended up dead broke and in prison because she refused to betray clients, who included President Giscard d'Estaing, not to mention cabinet ministers, industrialists, shipowners, aristocrats, and yours truly.

See what I mean? It is the opposite of journalists, who have neither discretion nor guts, while great courtesans have always had both. And this traditionally has granted some of them considerable power.

For though in common usage a harlot is a woman whose function is to provide a man with sexual pleasure, in times past prostitutes serving courtly, wealthy, upper-class clientele were often able to act to effect results in the world at large. This was so even back in ancient Greece.

Although Aspasia ran what was deemed a disreputable business, training young "hetaerae," she was regarded as a philosopher and politician.

Socrates, in fact, came to see her with his disciples, and in the end she effectively ran the country. As Plutarch wrote in his *Life of Pericles*, "She told Pericles what to do and he did it."

The French, of course, excelled in the sexual liberation of women while the Americans were still burning so-called witches. From Madame de Pompadour to Madame du Barry, both of whom serviced Louis XV, to the Belle Époque to Madame Claude.

Grandes horizontales were known for their responsibility to their wealthy patrons, taking pride in their vocation and wielding their power judiciously. (That, again, is more than I can say for the pompous, self-important, and sycophantic journalists at Bezos's *Washington Post* and Sulzberger's *New York Times*.)

Alas, such courtesans are no more, as discretion is no more. In their place we have wealthy social climbers, or aspirants to that status, for whom quality is equated only with price. And being born into the upper classes today assures nothing better.

The *grandes horizontales* of old were also better educated than those today who give it away, as well as better judges of character.

Which brings us back to the wonderful and much-missed Madame Claude.

One day when I was still in exile, I received a telephone call from my father. He wanted me back in Paris pronto. He needed me to entertain certain Indonesian generals and assorted biggies about to arrive in the City of Light.

"This is important shipping business," said Dad. "Don't fuck it up."

The crux of it was that the Indonesians were handing out the contracts for Pertamina, the national oil company, and they expected to be suitably entertained. Which meant women.

Lots of them. Indonesians are among the horniest people on the planet, and the richer and more powerful they are, the randier.

"Oh, yes," added Daddy, "how good is your golf? The general likes golf and girls."

Golf in my book is for sissies—I'd lately taken up martial arts in a near-fanatical way—but on landing in Paris off I went to Saint-Cloud for some cramming.

At the same time, in collaboration with Madame Claude, I set about assembling a team of girls that Jack Warner and Darryl Zanuck would have given their false teeth to have under contract. The deal with Claude was that they would accept no monetary favors from the general or his entourage, the remuneration coming from our side—I paying out of my own pocket.

General Ibnu Sutowo, head of Pertamina, proved to be small, tough, dignified, and no fool. But happily he was unfamiliar with Madame Claude and her operation.

So, for that matter, was my father, who spent little time in the French capital. It was one of the few lies I ever put across him, and it would be years before I fessed up.

The only hitch was my first wife. Our marriage was of recent vintage, and when she saw the collection of girls—passed off as "friends and acquaintances"—she went bananas. But even this worked in our favor, as it helped convince the general it was all for real.

After one week of debauch, General Ibnu was madly in love and the contracts were signed, the deal so outrageously in our favor that Indonesian President Suharto soon banned foreign companies operating Indonesian ships.

But there was a postscript—two of them, in fact.

Having been around a long time among the rich and infamous, one really does know all the secrets. And, yes, it is true that many very high-end hookers, perhaps half of them, end up with very rich men. In the ex-Soviet Union's case, it's ninety-nine to one in favor of the hookers. But the rumors about Madame Claude's girls are particularly vivid, and I must say that these have been somewhat exaggerated. While most certainly married well enough, only a couple struck it fabulously rich. And one of these returned to Jakarta after a weeklong junket in Paris.

My other P.S.? When my father returned to Athens, he told my mother that I was not as worthless as he thought. "The little one has talent, he isn't as big an idiot as he acts. You should see the girls he came up with. I wonder how he convinced them to jump into bed with those monkeys."

SIX

Great Men Have Great Appetites

IT IS no secret that the so-called Casanova syndrome is in disrepute. In books, films, and plays, lotharios are the whipping boys. If Dante put the seducer in the eighth circle of hell, today's joyless feminists, labeling him genus reptilian, would toss him straight in the fire.

Needless to say, this is most unfortunate, and the result of serious misunderstandings and misconceptions.

I harken back to the wiser once-upon-a-time when the title Casanova was a badge of honor. For what it implied, and still does, was not only style, but graciousness, generosity of spirit, and honorable behavior in the world at large.

The real McCoy, the original, Giacomo Girolamo Casanova, lived a life that I would gladly give my own for. I am not talking about his conquests—he had only 122 in his lifetime, a figure that puts him, at best, in the second or third division. No, the reason Casanova was a great man is what someone described as his "plurality of worlds." He was an actor, an inventor, a violinist, an author of more than twenty books, a playwright, a spy, and many other things.

He discussed poetry with Voltaire, advised Empress Catherine of Russia on how to reform the calendar, and even wrote a sci-fi novel long before anyone else had even imagined the genre. He also discussed engineering and finance with Frederick the Great of Prussia—who was homosexual, and came on to him—no luck—and met Mozart in Prague in 1787, the year Wolfgang presented *Don Giovanni* for the first time. It was an evening when the legendary real and mythical seducers came under the same roof.

Great men have great appetites, and Casanova was a great all-rounder. He was generous and elegant, romantic and brave.

And while first and foremost he was a seducer, he was the antithesis of the crude Hollywood producer. He did not merely admire and respect women, he made their happiness his life's work. "He undressed them as if they were his superiors," wrote one of his biographers. He never ruined a woman. If anything he was a fool for love.

Throughout my life most of my closest friends have been great womanizers, and I say with certainty that there is nobody to whom I would rather entrust my life than a "swordsman." Who else would have the daring, the persistence, and the cunning essential to getting one out of tough scrapes in times of crisis? Men schooled in seduction understand the difference between bravery and foolhardiness, considered action and rashness. Theirs is a boldness tempered by wisdom—which the philosophers define as the essence of manly virtue.

History shows that such men, imbued with an understanding of human nature in all its vast variety and endless contradictions, have made our greatest statesmen. Louis XIV and Louis XV were both very randy, and both were great kings, advised respectively by Mesdames de Pompadour and du Barry; their hapless successor Louis XVI, who never fooled around, could hardly get it together, and look how he ended up. (If only he'd had a wise bedmate to advise him!)

Talleyrand was both the greatest statesman and the greatest lover France has ever produced. Napoleon may have called him "a shit in a silk stocking," but unlike the emperor, he was around at the end, having salvaged a measure of French dignity and along the way seduced three generations of the Duchess of Dino, granny, mother, and daughter. It takes character to do that, as it took character to save France at the Congress of Vienna, playing with the weakest of hands. Coincidentally, his illegitimate son, Count de Flahaut, was the lover of three queens, including Napo's sister and step-daughter. Three was a lucky number for the Talleyrand family.

Talleyrand's great rival, Austria's Prince Metternich, was also no slouch between the sheets. He seduced everyone—the wife of a Russian general, the nieces of his emperor, even the sister of his archenemy Napoleon. He had two duchesses as mistresses, one of whom, Princess Bagration, cost him Bavaria when he overslept with her as the winners were redistributing real estate. When informed, he sighed and said, "But she was worth it." Now that's what I call character! Let's have more erotomaniacs and fewer hypocrites!

Napo himself was one of the many great military commanders who also knew how to maneuver in the bedroom. Among his successors, General Christian de Castries, while as a top commander in Indochina he may have been less than illustrious on the battlefield, nonetheless flashed his swordsman's élan by naming his soon-to-be overrun outposts at Dien Bien Phu after his many mistresses, Dominique, Elianne, Gabrielle, Beatrice, Isabelle. Among Americans, General Patton was a fabled womanizer, as hard-charging tank commanders are bound to be.

These were men in full, and there's nothing like reading beautifully written sagas of their bravery and reflecting on the human predicament. If Ava Gardner and Betty Grable were alive and asked me to join them for a threesome, it would be just the thing to take along a copy of *Normandy '44* for a quick read between sessions. (And if that dates me, I'd be pleased to substitute Jennifer, as in Lawrence, and Keira as in Knightley, to complement the manly heroics.) (Speaking of living vicariously, on a recent tour of the battlefields of northern France, I climbed on a Tiger tank, and a French woman screamed at me to get off. I answered her in perfect but German-accented French that I had been on it eighty years earlier and was just reliving my youth.)

On the other side of the ledger, there are leaders who are doggedly faithful, most of whom . . . let's just say I well remember what my father said to my brother and me the beautiful spring morning he took us to the airport at Athens to say goodbye to Constantine and Nadine Tsaldaris, the then-Greek prime minister and his wife, who were off for their first official visit to the United States. I was terribly impressed by the military bigwigs who were present, but also by the fact that it was Mrs. Tsaldaris, the most formidable of ladies, who did most of the talking. Afterward, driving back, my father told us that Tsaldaris was a good and honest man, but that he wouldn't last because he was weak. "Never trust an uxorious husband, especially when he's a politician," was the way the old boy put it. Sure enough, Tsaldaris soon fell from power, and the Olive Republic wouldn't have a strong leader for a decade.

I remembered this many years afterward when I met the worst ever example of uxoriousness among occupants of the White House, Jimmy Carter. The peanut farmer was the nicest of men. Not only did he cheat on his wife only in his mind, he permitted Rosalynn to attend cabinet meetings, and allowed her to speak. Needless to say, he was a disastrous president. Ditto George W.

Bush, the other architect of the ongoing Middle East calamity. On the other side of the pond, Ted Heath, among the all-time weakest PMs, never cheated on anyone only because he never had anyone to cheat on.

There are exceptions to the general rule, of course—in my lifetime, notably Churchill (too English) and Truman (too Midwestern)—but it holds true to an astonishing extent not just in politics and diplomacy, but in any endeavor that relies on daring and independence of judgment.

Among the many literary lady killers, no one traded more obviously on the charisma of creativity than Byron, who like Erroll Flynn had it all. But the short, one-eyed, crippled poet and patriot Gabriele D'Annunzio likewise managed to seduce every beautiful woman of his time. And even Chateaubriand, a disagreeable, 5'4", bandy-legged morose type with a hump on his back, had mistresses flocking to him. His fame certainly helped, but mainly he caressed them with his talk. He even cheated on his greatest love, Juliette Récamier, hymned as the loveliest woman in the world. Good for you, François-René.

As for composers, again the list is too long to compile, but suffice to say it would start with Franz Liszt, who might as well have been all four Beatles rolled into one.

Mozart's co-creator of *Don Giovanni*, the librettist Lorenzo Da Ponte, was a Venetian Jew who was eventually exiled by the Inquisitors for loose morals—i.e., seducing women left and right. He ended up in Brooklyn of all places, giving Italian lessons to upper-class New York women.

Don Giovanni is viewed near universally as a great sinner—the opera's original title was *Il Dissolute Punito*. Yet the Don Giovanni Da Ponte bequeathed to the ages is not among literature's most memorable characters because he was a heartless seducer; he was not. He adored women, and they adored him in return. True, he could go too far, he should not have killed the Commendatore, but what the hell?—life was cheaper back then. Far more meaningful is that, when he's on the run and the faithful Leporello asks him why can't he cool it for a while, the Don replies that it would be "unfair to other women if he were loyal only to one." Now that's the opposite of a cad. That's what I call a great man.

The Forties and Fifties were the golden days of international playboys. I was lucky enough to catch the end of it, and I have tried to do my bit to keep the noble tradition alive. Back then a playboy had to be first of all a man's man: physically tough and ready to defend his turf, a sportsman, as well as one who always treated a woman like a lady.

Like my father.

I was always close to my father, even more so in his later years, and there's not a day that goes by without my thinking of him and being proud. Indeed, after my scrape with British justice, it took me five years to write my prison book because I didn't want to hurt him with the truth. It was just as I'd decided finally to come clean that he passed away.

I lost my beloved father on the morning of July 14, 1989, when he dropped dead getting out of bed—he could not bear living through the 200th anniversary of the French Revolution. When my mother phoned to tell me, the news didn't register right away because I was still drunk from the night before. When it did, I broke down for probably the first time in more than forty years. I was not ashamed to do so, although he would have hated it.

In addition to all the rest, my father epitomized the conviction that a healthy adulterer ought to be able to carry on without destroying his marriage or family relationships. He used to sail around the Saronic Gulf in his whites with a ball and chain standard flying from his main mast. It meant "wife on board," which really meant: When I drop anchor in some nearby port, local talent should stay away. Dad was famous for flying that ensign, because he loved partying with loose women on his boat.

But during the rare occasions my mother would come on board, he didn't want to embarrass her with the inevitable visitors. After his death, when I would drop anchor at different islands, people would ask what happened to the flag. "Unlike my father, I am monogamous," I'd lie, and they'd invariably answer, "If only you could be half the man he was."

I have now been married to the mother of my children for over fifty years. Is ours an open marriage? Of course not. Over that long period there have understandably been complications with various women.

Some claimed to be expecting, others demanded moolah for the time they wasted with me.

But here's the thing—I never had any lasting troubles, and not a single woman ever went to the gutter press. Was I lucky? Not at all.

Because like my father, I have always chosen to go after a certain type of woman, the type who would rather die than sing to a gossip columnist.

The trick, you see, is to cuckold gents and to sleep with ladies.

Ergo, I've had a charmed life, including the greatest mother of children that it is possible to have.

My father's funeral was fitting in every respect. The high and mighty all came, including the head of government, the prime minister, and most of parliament, among other notables. But so did the men and women who had once worked for him on his vessels and in his factories, and ordinary people who had no connection with him at all. I was proud to be his son.

Fittingly, just as they lowered Father into the family crypt, a beautiful young girl appeared and threw in a flower.

Afterward, I saw her, and hesitated. No, I thought, I can't pick up a girl at my father's funeral.

But I was very close to it. "I saw what you did," I said. "It was a very noble, touching gesture. Who are you?"

She replied, "You know who I am."

And I realized: of course, father's latest girlfriend. Another nineteen-year-old.

SEVEN

We're in the Age of the Cad

LEST THERE be any confusion—which these days the enemies of traditional manhood are all too eager to spread—let's be doubly and triply clear about the distinction between the honorable men who embrace the Casanovan creed and the sleazy types who will take advantage of the fairer sex at every opportunity. There is a name for these, once in common parlance but too little used today: cad. It is defined by my *Cambridge Dictionary* as "a man who behaves badly or dishonestly, especially to women."

Sadly, we are living in the age of the cad.

How so? Obviously, there have always been odious men who preyed upon the weaker sex. And of course that was especially true of men with great power. Jack L. Warner was the prototype of the Hollywood swaggering bully and sexual predator, his daily use of the casting couch making Harvey Weinstein seem like a monk in comparison. As President Warren Harding fathered a child by his mistress while in the White House, and Grover Cleveland also had a bastard on his résumé. FDR continued his philandering even from a wheelchair. And, needless to say, JFK had a different woman every afternoon.

The difference was that none of it was common knowledge, and if it had been, it would have been curtains for those involved. Back in the better world before the 1960s, women held men in the public sphere up to standards of character and behavior; men accepted the arrangement and held the line.

Yes, there was more than a little hypocrisy in this, the biological imperative being what it is. But the female-enforced code of honorable male behavior served the vital purpose of promoting stable families. Not incidentally it was a model vigorously reinforced by the Hollywood studios in movie couples from William Powell and Myrna Loy to Doris Day and Rock Hudson, as well as in the family TV situation comedies of the Fifties so scornfully derided today by the left. Lies they indeed may have been, but comforting and very useful ones. Men aspired to live up to women's hopes for them, even as the supposed contented domesticity of the nation's leaders also served as a model for ordinary men and women.

America, with its Christian traditions written in stone, had always been different from any other Western country; more naïve in this respect, perhaps, but in consequence better off for it. More moral. We Greeks are brought up seeing adultery as a game in which we seek to excel, Don Juan and all that. But in America it was recognized as a source of larger corruptions, and the heads of the country knew to keep themselves on a higher level than, say, yours truly.

Now? All that's down the drain. Hollywood sneers at traditional mores, shamelessly endorsing the worst instincts of both sexes, when it's not actually undermining the very idea of normal biological sex. And of course in the last thirty years, the nation's leaders have followed suit, turning millions of those who grew up in better, more hopeful times into hardened cynics. Rather than revered, or even respected, those in high office today are more likely to be playground punch lines.

But even that doesn't quite tell it. While cads come in various forms and guises, the most dangerously insidious is the man of superior intelligence who uses it not to exalt but in pursuit of selfish short-term satisfaction, the consequences be damned. Indeed, the greatest cad in recent American history was not above turning millions of his own supporters into rank hypocrites in his shameless efforts to save his own skin.

For a long time, I actually hesitated to write about Bill Clinton's behavior. Taki attacking an adulterer is a bit like Rommel dismissing audacious tactics in battle as counterproductive. But Clinton and his feminist allies changed America forever. Gushing faux sincerity, this cad posing as a champion of women, eagerly fostered moral corruption in others. Sixties creature that he has always been, rather than do the manly thing and accept responsibility when caught red-handed—or, better yet, take the excuse to speak honestly about matters sexual, rather than treat his fellow citizens like children—he slobbered and dissembled in simpering self-pity. And the feminist harridans, far from holding him to account, rushed to excuse him.

This is how societies change, through the erosion of standards of public behavior that reflect character and honor. Whatever moral order there had been governing affairs between the sexes, now all was chaos.

It of course never shocked me that Clinton treated himself to Monica Lewinsky in the Oval Office. In the unlikely event of my being president, I would have done nothing else; though of course I would have chosen a beauty, and I certainly would have gone all the way. (A blow job is more pornography than sex—and even then, the Draft Dodger gave fellatio a bad name. I've heard of unsubtle approaches, but dropping one's trousers and telling a woman to kiss it is the romantic equivalent of a holiday in Zaire.)

In short, Clinton was the cad of cads—a vile weak-willed user all the more loathsome for his endless pretense to bottomless concern for womenkind.

Morality does not count, only spin does. This is the Clinton legacy.

Speaking of which . . . Monica Lewinsky. At an event some time back, that lady, which she is not, actually came up and offered her hand to the mother of my children, who shook it. "What was all that about?" I asked her. "Well, I didn't wish to be rude," said you know who. "At least she didn't kiss you," said yours truly, "or offer you a cigar."

Of course, having claimed victimhood (and put the onus for her problems way back when on the Republicans) Ms. Lewinsky now makes the rounds as an honest-to-goodness celebrity. And I suppose she really is a victim of sorts; having to blow Bill Clinton takes the act out of the human realm and into science fiction.

Though Clinton is indeed loathsome beyond compare, one must not give lesser cads a pass. For they are all over, in multiple varieties—from the corrupt and money-obsessed to the amoral and sociopathic—and each demeans women in his own way. (The Clintons, needless to say, check multiple boxes.)

Among the sociopaths, there has been no better example in my lifetime than Ted Kennedy, the very apotheosis of the philosophy "ladies last." Even now the word "Chappaquiddick" summons up horror. It is one (disreputable but understandable) thing to have a gruesome accident while under the influence and, perhaps, under certain circumstances, even to fib about it afterward; but it is of course something of an entirely different order to let a young woman suffocate while you run away to save your own miserable skin.

Which reminds me of something once said by Nigel Dempster, long England's numero uno gossip columnist. Asked how he slept at night having spent his day ruining people's lives, he did not hesitate a split second. "Easy," he answered. "I look at people's sex lives, especially those of prominent people, because the personal habits that manifest themselves only when observed up close are the ones that lead to detection of flaws that might influence public performance."

As for The Swimmer, he should have been locked away all those years he spent in the U.S. Senate doing damage to the country, not least in his disgusting knee-capping of infinitely better men like Robert Bork and Clarence Thomas.

Obviously, and not to repeat myself, I don't think that chasing girls is a bad thing. But Ted's antics careened way beyond disreputable even for a Kennedy. Not chastised in the wake of the Massachusetts murder, he continued to prey on young women even as he grew grotesquely fat.

The most infamous such episode might have been the "waitress sandwich" incident at Washington's La Brasserie, in which Kennedy acted as one end, and fellow Democrat sleaze Chris Dodd the other, with an unfortunate waitress named Carla Gaviglio, summoned to the senators' private table while their dates were in the bathroom, serving as the meat in between.

Among the grasping, avaricious cads, the worst of the many I have known might well be Thierry Roussel, who married Aristotle Onassis's daughter Christina. It would take a rare talent as a writer to describe Roussel accurately, without going to jail for criminal libel, since, alas, he is still among the living. When I first met him as a young man in Paris, he was merely another seedy show-off with the values of one who sells drugs to kids, but that was before Christina fell under his spell. Though her wise father distrusted him, Roussel was living the life of Riley in expensive resorts around the world. All well and good, many men have done the same. But then things took a tragic turn. Christina was thirty-seven when she was found by her maid in a bathtub in Buenos Aires, dead of a heart attack. But she must have known her days were numbered because three months before, having at last gotten the cad's number, she'd made a new will to ensure Roussel would not get hold of their daughter Athina's assets, at the time between one and two billion. But that didn't stop him from trying to ensure that his daughter's inheritance should be controlled solely by him. He went so far as to threaten to move with the child to France where the taxes would cost the estate a small fortune annually. To keep it brief, a suitable settlement was reached, and he has lived very, very well ever since. One can only speculate about the quality of Athina's childhood. Now if that isn't a modern Greek tragedy, I don't know what is.

A potential Roussel rival as Europe's most loathsome cad was fellow Frenchman Jean-Paul Sartre. While the existentialist posed as an infracaninophile—or champion of the underdog—in real life he treated women like the proverbial dirt and showed as much tenderness as Lavrentiy Beria. Nonetheless, he got more than his share of you-know-what. Why? Because internationally renowned peddlers of his brand of bullshit make leftist women swoon and go all shaky at the knees, never mind how lousy the lay. (And Sartre was one of the worst. Apparently, he could only get it up with two women, and then just for a little while.)

Other cads are of the kiss-and-tell kind, which is to say, they violate the trust that should be a sacred element in every meaningful liaison between willing partners. I have known many such, more than a few of whom have put their betrayal between covers of a book. The director Roger Vadim, a man I knew well, made multiple tidy sums by telling all about his exes Brigitte Bardot, Jane Fonda, and Catherine Deneuve. Which did not surprise me, as Vadim was that type from the get-go. Nor does it surprise me that he was Jane Fonda's guru for a long time, Fonda being as phony as she is.

Then there is Eddie Fisher, the man Elizabeth Taylor dumped for Richard Burton. Fisher was a horrid little man who used to sing horrid little songs, but he came into his own, as they say in Hollywood, when he described in his book how he went to bed with Merle Oberon while her penultimate husband was in the next room. Although I like to think I have a pretty strong stomach, reading Fisher's pathetic prose did make me feel queasy. What I really wanted to do was punch that indiscreet shit in the nose, only I imagined, and it didn't take much imagination, that that would have cost me a fortune.

One thing that has always amazed me about film stars of the fairer sex is the low quality of husbands they're more often than not saddled with. I guess it's because no self-respecting man would marry someone who spends all day rolling in the hay with another man while hundreds of randy extras are looking on. Whatever the reason, one thing is for sure. There is as much honor and dignity among Hollywood husbands as there is compassion in Tehran.

This gets me to Peter Holm, a Swedish ham once married to Joan Collins. He got £250,000 for spilling the beans about the *Dynasty* star, which is certainly not as bad as what Judas did a couple of thousand years ago, but definitely along the same lines. But not satisfied with 250 big ones, Holm also demanded millions for having been married to Joan for a mere thirteen months.

I must confess that when I read of Holm's demands, I whistled to myself that well-known aria from *South Pacific*, "This nearly was mine," before thinking the better of it. For, of course, I myself had once been Joan Collins's boyfriend.

Not that this was widely known. So I was surprised when some time after the appearance of Holm's tome, a friend told me over lunch he knew all about Joan and me.

"Don't believe everything you hear," said I. "Why do you think so?" "It's right there, in her book," he told me.

And sure enough it was. As soon as the lunch was over I grabbed a taxi and headed for the closest bookshop down market enough to have Joan's *Past Imperfect* on sale. Her version of the time we spent together was pretty much the way I remembered it, except that she had Nicky Hilton and me fighting in El Morocco over her, when in fact it was the Blue Angel (and I also had fought over her with a man named George DeWitt).

Plus there was another small detail in her book involving an older gentleman.

Back in 1957 I used to get up every morning quite early, just before lunch in fact, eat breakfast and then head for the tennis courts, where I would spend most of the afternoon. Joan would lunch with friends, or go shopping. One day a sudden downpour canceled the tennis early, and I headed back to the hotel. While entering I noticed Joan having lunch in the grill with this gentleman. I knew him very well, but had no idea she did at all, and was appreciative of the fact that he would take the time to keep her company. I also noticed she was wearing a diamond pin in the shape of an anchor.

In her book, the older man was never named, therefore I won't name him either. But because it was so long ago, I will note that at the time there were more women wearing jewels with a maritime theme around Athens than there were freeloaders at Aspinall's.

Not to worry, Joanie, this is as far as I'll ever go.

Of course, there are cads in many other realms, and also in other sexual guises. Leonard Bernstein, for example. Dimitri Mitropoulos was Greece's greatest conductor, a musical genius who has been sadly neglected. Bernstein was Salieri to Dimitri's Mozart. A sometime protégé of the Greek, Bernstein repaid the debt in 1948 by revealing Mitropoulos's homosexuality to the departing director of the Boston Symphony, Serge Kousseviztky, a homophobe. It was a post Dimitri craved, and although the Judas did not get the job, someone else, Charles Munch, did. By the way, Mitropoulos was no drag-ass queen, à la Lenny himself.

But the majority of cads are simply users, exploiting a woman for what they can get, then dropping them when they're no longer of use.

And they can belong as easily to those who pass through the world as successful and even celebrated as to those semi-permanently on barstools at the local bar.

Take, for instance, the fellow my second wife was seeing when I met her in Paris. She was all of seventeen at the time, a beautiful young Austrian princess playing hooky from school during the '68 riots and visiting the barricades every night in the Left Bank. He was a left-leaning lawyer by the name of François Moreuil, and like most left-leaning people he liked the good life. At the time he was a fixture at places like Castel's and Regine's, dancing the night away while seething with revolutionary fervor. Fine with me. While he was going out with the girl who eventually became the mother of my children, I would invite him for dinner in order to get near her, and he always accepted because it was a free meal. He and I used to argue over politics and, at times, over girls, and in between I managed to make an impression on his girlfriend, Alexandra. Eventually Alexandra dropped Moreuil for me. Although supposedly a gentleman, the Frenchman did not react like one. He waited outside her house and tried to make up for the rather pathetic performance of the French army against the German one in World War II. Needless to say, that brash action meant the end of a beautiful friendship. But not to worry about Moreuil. He went on to marry one of the richest girls in France and live in a chateau, extremely happily. Incidentally, he also dropped his lefty politics.

Moreuil comes to mind not only because of my own fortuitous association with him, but because he was connected by marriage to a far more loathsome member of the cad species—the renowned French writer Romain Gary. Because before his little flirtation with the future Mrs. Taki, Moreuil was briefly married to Jean Seberg, the all-American looking kid from Iowa who would die so sordidly at the age of forty.

Seberg's story is a full-scale American tragedy. She was discovered at seventeen by the director Otto Preminger, a man who made up for his lack of talent by bullying people under his control. (I insulted him a couple of times in public places, but he never chose to return the compliment.) Anyway, like most bullies he knew how to pick his spots, and Seberg—an idealistic, beautiful, healthy, and intelligent young girl—was an easy target. After the failure of the film about Joan of Arc for which he'd found her, he put all the blame on her, tyrannizing her, berating her in public, and doing his best to destroy the little natural talent she had.

When she finally had had enough, Seberg ran off with François Moreuil to Paris. She was already known there despite the bad notices. With a good director, Jean-Luc Godard, she made *Breathless* and was soon a star. Moreuil was happy to bask in her limelight, but it takes more than the bright lights of Paris to remove the Iowa Puritanism from a seventeen-year-old. Seberg rightly felt used by him and dropped him.

Now enters the real villain of the piece, for her replacement was Gary. If there ever was an egomaniacal phony, Romaine Gary was it. He too was an armchair leftist, and for kicks he manipulated his movie-star wife into becoming a rebel, and she proved dangerously attracted to political terrorism, violence, and sexual excess. Don't forget, this was Paris during the Sixties, and Gary and revolution were very much in vogue. When he eventually began to push her to form a *liaison dangereuse*, he was not prepared for her small-town American stubbornness. She ran off with the various black revolutionaries he brought to the house.

Eventually, she settled on one. The marriage broke up and after the excesses of the Sixties were over, Jean found herself bereft and hooked: on drugs, criminal men, and outdated revolutionary ideas. She became a zombie, running naked through the streets and injecting herself publicly. Her once-beautiful looks were gone before she reached thirty. She ended up with an Arab pimp. And one cold day she was found dead inside a car, naked except for a blanket. She had been dead for over a week without anyone missing her.

After her death Romain Gary once again exploited her. He called a press conference and charged that the FBI was responsible for her depression and eventual death. This was never proved although she had been under FBI surveillance after her fundraising for the Black Panthers.

If there is a moral to be drawn it is this: Letting your daughter go out with Hollywood types or radical chics, or cads of any kind, could prove fatal.

EIGHT

When Journalists Were Actual Pimps

OF COURSE, there is one highly prominent member of the cad brotherhood, political division aside, to whom I've so far given a near-pass. This is because his is a more complicated case.

I met Senator John Kennedy one year before he became president, at a party thrown by Alice Topping, a society dame of the time. The first and lasting impression was of his charisma and good looks. He was thirty-nine. The room was full of beautiful women, but he took a couple of minutes to ask me about school and my plans for the future. It was the sort of thing most politicians do, but with a difference. Because there was also some man-to-man chitchat and jokes about our wandering eyes.

Where Clinton is everything I despise in the modern feminized man—the great empathizer, given to bear hugs and able to summon up tears at will—Kennedy was the real thing, starting with his handshake. My respect and admiration for men who have honorably served their country is bottomless, and one was the hero of PT-109, the other a Draft Dodger. (Worse, Clinton charted the way for chief executives to follow; Bush and Cheney between them took more draft deferments than I've known hookers.) Moreover, so stoic was JFK in the face of constant pain that no one but his intimates was even aware of it.

He was, in short, a fit representative of his more manly times. It is fitting that, unlike Clinton, JFK only used cigars to smoke.

Still, though he had infinitely higher standards, it is undeniable that the martyred Kennedy was nearly the match of the Arkansas hick in his ungentlemanly way with the fairer sex.

We know this now following decades of after-action reports in the media, but of course no one had an inkling then. Well, no, not no one—everyone in the press knew. Indeed, anyone who has read about the Kennedy years knows that the one figure who stands out as a Kennedy flunky was *Washington Post* editor Ben Bradlee, who not only covered up JFK's philandering (as well he should have), but also his bungling in Cuba and in Vienna, not to mention Kennedy's complicity in the murder of South Vietnamese President Diem. Watergate would make Bradlee a household name—in the movie he was played with élan by Jason Robards—but to me he was no better than a pimp. Literally. Because Bradlee did procure women for JFK, even going so far as to offer up his own wife (his second one, now deceased, not the present widow) to his randy friend. Needless to say, this was something Kennedy courtiers such as Arthur Schlesinger also preferred to overlook, along with every hack during and since. But in Taki's book, pimps are pretty low down in the bad guy category. Laying one's wife to the prince's bed might have been a Victorian perversion, but never before had Americans done that sort of thing.

I was once invited to the White House by another Kennedy pimp, the fashion designer Oleg Cassini, but turned down the invitation because I knew what JFK needed from me, namely my then-girlfriend.

On other occasions, I had more direct experience with the president's special way with the ladies.

At the time I was friendly with a pretty French girl, Danielle Pons, niece of the French ambassador to the United States. Her uncle, Herve Alphand and his wife Nicole were the best party-givers in town, and great favorites of JFK and Jackie.

But my days as a Washington embassy regular ended as a result of my friend Danielle's brief fling with JFK. A regular visitor to the White House during the fling, Danielle fell rather hard as it started winding down. Being young and headstrong, she'd start making a scene when, having serviced the president, she was asked to leave the executive mansion. Her uncle asked me to give her a lecture, which I did, but when that didn't work, JFK finally simply told her it was all over. Danielle was then struck by the notion that she might be able to get him back by giving a small press conference on the lawn of the embassy. The next thing she knew, her uncle had her on a plane to Paris, heavily sedated, where she woke up among her family with a note attached to her dressing gown that read: "Gardez en France à tout prix."

But the story has a happy ending. In short order, she would again be having a very good time in Paris with young Taki. Her favorite song was "Itsy Bitsy Teenie Weenie Yellow Polkadot Bikini."

A year or so later, in 1962, I was going out with Anne Ford, whose papa owned a car company by the same name. An all-American girl, she too had spent time in Paris, but was no linguist. When someone said "Bonjour" to her, she could only answer, "Daddy's in Detroit." Anyway, one night in New York, in the Carlyle Hotel, she came into the room where I was waiting looking all flushed and disheveled. It took me a long time to coax the story from her. Eventually, she told me her attacker was John F. Kennedy himself. She had gone into the presidential suite of the Carlyle for a drink and right off the bat he jumped on her, stopping only when she threatened to tell her father. I imagine Kennedy must have thought, "There goes Michigan." So he never got rough.

I made sympathetic noises and held her close and said "There, there," but didn't believe a word. Who knows what really happened, but very few girls said no to JFK.

Needless to say, there is much more. The tragic Marilyn was known as an inveterate scribbler—she kept diaries of everything and everybody she came into contact with. Yet nothing was found after her death. But there is a policeman who swears that Kennedy and his friends tried to silence Monroe by offering her pills and other sedatives that fateful night. And, too, there are hints that Bobby and JFK had contact with Sam Giancana, a well-known Mafia leader, and for me the hints are good enough. I knew Sam Giancana as Sam Moody. I had been introduced to him by Peter Lawford, and had heard the actor and the mobster talk fondly of the Kennedys and reminisce about past shenanigans with the "first family."

Needless to say, the Kennedys enjoyed privileges that ordinary mortals, and mortal politicians, could only aspire to. The president of ABC News, Kennedy friend Roone Arledge, once canceled a program insiders said proved almost beyond a reasonable doubt that Bobby Kennedy was in Los Angeles the night MM died, and furthermore that he'd had a lot to do with her death. The program included on-air interviews with people who said they'd bugged Marilyn's house on the orders of Jimmy Hoffa, the gangster leader of the Teamsters Union that Bobby had sworn to send to jail, and that too went down the proverbial drain. The Camelot myth had to be protected at all costs.

Still, I must admit that throughout that period, even knowing all the little Greek boy did, he too remained somewhat under

JFK's spell. He was, after all, a very good-looking man, with enormous charm, who'd fought for his country. And even now, knowing all we do, his personal charisma is undisputed.

However, my father never shared that feeling. He had rooted hard for Richard Nixon in 1960, both of us had, and it is an election I remember as if it were yesterday. Daddy had given a lot of moolah to RN, and as they say, he had plans. Throughout the night we sat up in the Sherry-Netherland Hotel drinking and hoping Nixon would make it. It wasn't until Mayor Daley of Chicago manipulated the Illinois vote that JFK claimed victory, a typical Kennedy victory—hollow, unfair, and paid for.

I met Nixon soon after that, and renewed my friendship with him years later. He wrote to me while I was in Pentonville, which was both encouraging and compassionate, showing a tender side of the man that has rarely been written about, and he had me to dinner in his house when I came out.

The truth is, Nixon was guilty mainly of the one crime politicians in America cannot afford to commit—a lack of charisma and charm. He was indeed (in the Nixonian phrase) kicked around with sanctimonious impunity, and done ultimately in, by the very people in the Fourth Estate who turned a blind eye and a deaf ear knowing the Kennedys were up to far worse while in the White House.

I never saw JFK in person again. Like everyone else alive and out of a crib on November 22, 1963, I remember it well. I was going to 21 for lunch, and 52nd Street traffic had stopped while people listened to car radios. We all know the rest. What people were not aware of was the unquestionable sleight of hand worked by Jackie while arranging the details of the funeral, having even rehearsed her little boy's salute as his father's cortège passed. Despite her Medea-like rage and grief, she went over the list of those invited to attend and added her personal favorites, including Ari Onassis and J.D. Salinger.

To her credit, the widow quickly put some distance between herself and the rowdy Irish bunch of her husband's brood. Except for Bobby Kennedy, he was different from the rest. Though perceived as the realist to JFK's romantic, in reality he was the romantic to the realist his elder brother was.

For her part, Jackie wanted center stage and she got it in spades, five years later becoming Mrs. Onassis. But one graceful act she never got credit for was the letter in blue stationery she wrote to the widow of Officer Tippit, the policeman Oswald murdered in cold blood by pumping four bullets into him before going to the movie house where he was finally arrested. She wrote how she worried that in their grief for the president, Americans might forget the officer's death in the line of duty, but that she (Jackie) never would. That's as graceful and profoundly moving as it gets.

In any case, Jackie made sure the history police held firm, with Schlesinger, Richard Goodwin, and Ted Sorensen playing leading roles. How good or bad a president was Kennedy really? Let's put it this way:

He was an insecure president, but with great charisma and personal courage. If greatness is to be found, it only lies in comparison to the awful LBJ and George W. Bush, and of course William Jefferson Clinton who, if in this single instance is to be believed, took the charming JFK as his inspiration when he was a young hick.

Can one even imagine JFK buddying up to the inexorable Jeffrey Epstein à la Clinton? Well, perhaps, but he wouldn't have needed to—either for the girls or the campaign cash.

Needless to say, JFK never faced any questions about his own behavior with women. But the guess here is that if he had, he'd have handled them with characteristic aplomb, which is to say charmingly, and with humor. Certainly not by questioning the definition of "is."

Of course, unlike the JFK era, there are no heroes these days, just degrees of clay feet. Nothing anyone does is surprising anymore—so much so, I'm always surprised by people's surprise. One of the last to fall was Tiger Woods, back in 2009, but that was only because his image had been glossed to a Kennedyesque sheen. Still, it was a near universal surprise that he'd been cheating on his wife with reckless abandon. What universe were people living in? This is today's world. Billionaire sports stars pick up babes as often as Bill Clinton lies, which is incessantly, be it tennis, golf, and especially basketball and football. There seems hardly a player in the NBA that doesn't have numerous children with different women. One of them has nine, but pays for only three of them for some strange reason. His case is being reviewed by the courts. This is what comes with the wholesale abandonment of standards at the top.

Incidentally, compared with Bill Clinton's tarts, Tiger's were of slightly better quality, which is not saying much. The prettiest of the lot, Rachel Uchitel, had been at school with my daughter, which when I learned of it caused me some distress. When I tried to talk to my little girl about her, with my customary degree of solicitude, I was cut off at the pass. "Daddy, stop it!"

NINE

How Feminism Ruined Everything for Everyone

It was a good life I was living then, and it's a pity to sully an account of it by going into greater depth about a subject so depressing as feminism. But this bane of all humankind is, alas, inescapable.

I of course saw it for what it is from the start, a war against biological reality (not to mention human satisfaction). So over the ensuing decades I have watched with some alarm as it metastasized from a subject of ready mockery to a set of sacrosanct precepts held beyond reproach by polite society.

Back in the 1970s, before the disease had come to full maturity—its chief advocates invariably being physically as well as intellectually objectionable—I was sometimes recruited to provide an opposing view.

I was good at it, which is to say far better than my opponents.

Why? For the simple reason that I told the truth and they did not—and could not—since their movement is built on outrageous fictions.

For instance, toward the end of the decade, I was contacted by *The Phil Donahue Show*, then extremely popular, and offered a round-trip first-class ticket from Athens to Chicago in exchange for sixty minutes of my time. An anti-feminist article I'd written for *The American Spectator* under the heading "American Women Are Lousy Lovers," had caught their eye. In fact, the article had nothing whatsoever to do with the sexual act, it simply poked fun at grim feminists who see everything through a lens of power and conquest, as well as of their endless aggressive posturing and lack of femininity. Bob Tyrrell, the editor who'd suggested I write the piece, saw it as a sort of update on Helen Lawrenson's 1936 dissertation, "Latins Are Lousy Lovers." That is, it was largely tongue-in-cheek. But needless to say, Donahue's producers jumped at the title without ever bothering to read the piece.

Although training for the European karate championships at the time, I accepted. Donahue then had the largest daytime television audience in the world, proving yet again that there are more idiots in America than anywhere else. His challenge to debate my premises was irresistible.

How so? Because women generally recognize the truth when they hear it.

The show's format was simple. Donahue walked around the audience—who, I was told, usually waited two years for their seats—and chatted with them. Only in my case it was a bit different. They seated me on a stool in the middle and the audience was urged to throw questions at me. I was informed of this format just five minutes before going on the air, which was unnerving, as I was unprepared for the onslaught. But I was not about to argue, and I let it go at that.

In my *American Spectator* article I had suggested that the women's liberation movement had managed to turn out moral clones of the male chauvinists it despises. My advice to American women was to forget about becoming sensual and sexual through the ubiquitous instruction books and, as women are sensual by nature, simply let nature take its course. I also told them to stop measuring themselves by their supposed achievements, to stop being so driven, and to stop hating their sex organs. Last but not least, I advised them to emulate their European sisters who long ago discovered something vastly superior to the hate rhetoric against men—namely, manipulating the stronger sex and getting their way in the time-honored tradition of the ancient Greeks.

Despite the cheeky nature of the article, I was sincere in all of this. I do fervently believe that love between humans is not merely an indulgence in carnal pleasure. If it were purely a matter of mastering technique, I readily conceded the American feminists would be tops. In the same way as at the time they were into jogging or performing Jane Fonda's exercises.

Donahue, however, chose to read the more provocative stuff, most of it out of context. I didn't mind. Phil, as everyone called the star, was a nice looking man with premature gray hair and the kind of professional and contrived earnestness affected by hawkers in front of strip joints. He did at least allow me to defend myself, and was very generous in deferring to me.

During the course of the hour—that is, once I had been able to state my views in their entirety—it was obvious a lot of the women began to agree with me. Donahue didn't even seem to mind that. What he wanted was controversy and that he was getting. Afterward, the producer told me that the telephone was ringing off the hook.

In fact, after the show I also ran into Lana Turner, waiting her turn to sell her book. She was now a tiny old lady. "Boy, do I ever agree with what you say about these feminists," she growled at me when I wished her good luck. Ironically, if there ever was a person who was exploited by men and the system it was Miss Turner, yet she was far too feminine to hate all men.

It all ended badly for Donahue and well for yours truly, when after some needling I definitively showed him up as a wimpy ignoramus and hypocrite. The key moment came when I made my case for keeping a mistress but never divorcing my loyal wife. "Unlike you, Phil," said I, "we Europeans do not change wives for a new model, as though they were a car, every year. We put them on a pedestal, worship them, and have our fun on the side. Didn't you get rid of the mother of your five children last year for a new model?"

"You son-of-a-bitch," exploded Donahue, but the mostly middle-aged women began cheering for me.

Donahue fancied himself a model feminist, but of course that is exactly what he had done, the newer model being the actress/feminist-activist Marlo Thomas.

As a general rule, I try never to mix sex with politics. I learned it's a losing game back in the Fifties when the overthrow of Jacobo Arbenz of Guatemala by the CIA cost me a beautiful girl. Bella Arbenz hated the Yanks in general and the spooks in particular. One night in Paris, just as she had agreed to play house with me, like a fool I defended them. I could have legitimately pled ignorance—how was I supposed to know she was the deposed president's daughter? On the other hand, why get into it at all? As it was, not only did she throw me out, as I stood underneath her window begging to be allowed back in, she also flung some yellow liquid.

But the "silence is golden" rule goes out the window even faster when I begin to pick up signals that the girl's a feminist, or even so much as entertains stray feminist sympathies. Indeed, I seize every opportunity that comes my way to abuse women's libbers and to point out that feminism is a cruel hoax.

Quite simply, the notion that, superficial differences aside, the sexes are essentially the same is not merely an outrageous lie, it plays as haphazardly with the natural order and human affairs as any Greek god ever dared.

In short, feminism is an evil that can only lead to chaos and misery—as it so demonstrably has.

Before we get into the disheartening matter of the world as feminists have remade it—a subject I try to avoid to the maximum possible degree—let's take a moment to fondly recall the one that we have lost, the one where boys were boys and girls were girls and the twain met by happy mutual agreement. When that time is recalled today, it is likely to be via some feminist take on how awful things used to be, or increasingly, in reports of courtroom proceedings involving some allegation of sexual impropriety.

So let's start with one minor aspect of what ought to be a reality (and I daresay a healthy one) of male-female interaction, but which has now been declared illicit: the wolf whistle.

Once upon a more graceful time, before woke ruined men, women, and the Anglo-Saxon world in general, wolf-whistling was a standard issue (and harmlessly ineffectual) piece of equipment in the male arsenal, working-class division. Cops, firemen, and especially construction workers were expected to whistle at a passing pretty girl. Who among my age group will forget that wonderful Cartier-Bresson black-and-white photograph of a beautiful American girl in Rome being whistled at while running the gauntlet of Roman lotharios? What made the picture so memorable was the enormous smile on her face.

Yet I have a report of an English judge, one Geoffrey Kilfoil, who imposed a sentence of two weeks behind bars on a nineteen-year-old named Paul Powell for whistling at a knockout in his courtroom. The cavalier young Powell was in Kilfoil's courtroom as a spectator, lending moral support to a friend up for shoplifting, and the knockout, Alexa Hamley, twenty-two, was a juror in an unrelated case. According to witnesses, the illegal whistle was accompanied by a (presumably also illegal) sly wink, and it was perhaps this that roused the full fury of the male feminist judge. "Arrest this man at once!" he ordered, and five burly cops snapped to it, bringing the young man before the killjoy to be handed his fourteen days in the slammer. A sentence worthy of a Dickens novel.

Happily, there was an ending to the tale that also might have been penned by Dickens. An appeals court let young Powell loose after only two days in the cooler. More, far more, the lovely Miss Hamley gave a press conference in which she stated unequivocally that she enjoyed having men whistle at her because it "was only a way of saying I'm pretty." As soon as he was out of the slammer, the intrepid Mr. Powell drove twenty-five miles to her house, only to learn that his potential beloved, an aspiring model, was off on assignment. But he swore to keep trying.

Now there's a story to warm the cockles of a romantic's heart.

Good men everywhere cheered the outcome.

From such small things we of course may discern large ones, and I am certain that on reading this report, Taki was not the only one to ask: What have we come to? Why are males no longer encouraged—even permitted—to act like males and females like females?

Can anyone believe that American men will stand up to the Chinese when our leading universities and corporations are issuing guidebooks instructing that the very term "mankind" is no longer to be used?

Yet, I am one of the very few to have regularly posed this question publicly. So terrified are those who ought to be guardians of our cultural norms that they cower at the mere prospect of truth telling. They issue edicts from the seats of government, produce movies with radical feminist messages in Hollywood, and create television commercials where the women are the breadwinners while the men are at home pondering what detergent to use.

Yes, it is a dangerous world out there, with the cancelers lurking around every corner.

So let's again harken back to the common sense Fifties, my favorite decade. It couldn't have been a better time for young Taki. I was on the tennis circuit, traveling nonstop seeing the world, going out with beautiful women, and no matter how much I partied—and I partied nonstop—I was never tired or hungover. But above all, it was the times themselves that were good. Everyone knew right from wrong, truth from falsehood, who the good guys were—the Yankees—and that the Russkies were the bad guys. Young men were split between those who wore suits and ties and had short hair, and the "greasers," who had long, duck-tailed hair, blue suede shoes, and a go-screw-yourself attitude. But they knew they were men, as young women—who had full skirts, high heels, and perms—knew they were women. I belonged to the suit wearers but kinda liked the greasers' lack of respect. And the girls who went out with the greasers secretly liked us squares, as long as we weren't real squares but only pretended to be. Nature in all its glory.

Of course, the feminists saw to it the Fifties got a bad rap—sneered at by *bien-pensants* everywhere as a desert of dreary, inspiration-killing, anti-women uniformity.

A certain Virginia Nicholson produced a widely read book, *Perfect Wives in Ideal Homes*, that propagates the same lie that *The Stepford Wives* and other such rubbish has spread to such ill effect: that the last thing a man wanted back then was a clever woman. In my long life I've heard a hell of a lot of idiocy, but that takes the biscuit. I can't think of anyone I've ever met or heard of who wanted a dumb broad as a wife. It was Hollywood that made up the role of the dumb blonde, in films starring Marilyn Monroe, Jayne Mansfield, and Mamie Van Doren. And it's the pop scene that followed, with groupies hurling themselves at some pretty ugly men, that perpetuated the myth.

Nicholson also writes, accusingly, that according to surveys the chief aspiration of women in 1956 was to get married. And so what? Yes, a lot of women looked forward to having a family. Girls then regularly went out, got jobs, met the right boy, and had children. Again, what's the big deal? It's a description of social organization that worked well, far from perfect, but brought general contentment—which is to say, in most ways far better than the one we live under today. The man brought home the bacon, the woman took care of the house and the children, and what was wrong with that? It might even be called nature's way.

But this in no way suggests women then weren't smart, or interesting. When I entered university in September 1955, and took to visiting women's schools to chat up girls, most were studying history, English, or the liberal arts in general. I don't think I ever met one that was reading deportment, cookery, laundry skills, or embroidery.

Needless to say, it was Betty Friedan, a very smart but awfully ugly woman, who launched today's feminism in the sixties, with her book *The Feminine Mystique*, which claimed there was a fundamental sense of uneasiness, frustration, and a vague unhappiness that most women had trouble articulating. Society, according to Betty, had imposed a role on women they basically resented. She wrote that what she called "the feminine mystique," had succeeded "in burying millions of American women alive." Friedan became an overnight sensation. The women she interviewed to support her thesis reminded me a lot of highly decorated soldiers who are interviewed and prompted by reporters. "So you instantly realized that your platoon was about to be overrun, so you threw yourself up front . . ." says the hack. "Yeah, if you say so," answers the soldier. Men fight for their unit and react automatically to danger.

Their lives, and the lives of their buddies, do not flash before their eyes, and in Technicolor to boot, just before they act. Ditto for women being interviewed by other women about lost opportunities.

We men were portrayed as the big bad guys in the battle of the sexes. Not that very many believed it fifty years ago. But today we have been reduced to whimpering simps, collaborating in our own destruction. If Friedan was worried about the withering of women's minds by domesticity, what of us poor men today, battered nonstop by aggressive women who see lovemaking as rape and all men as potential rapists and murderers? I have never been a pincher or a groper and am very safe in taxis. But if I sometimes pay a lady a compliment, I don't expect to be called a pig for it.

Still, badly as it's all worked out for us, it is even worse for women. While men have been encouraged to no longer think of women as the fair and gentle sex—and thus no longer to be treated with care and respect, but simply as equals who are not quite equal enough—women are now encouraged to behave unnaturally in every sphere; that is, to be pushy and assertive and wholly unfeminine.

It is apparent at any social gathering where it is women who drive the conversation. Men who once would have gotten together and talked politics or sports are now only too eager to join the gals and natter on about children, or getting in touch with their emotions, or whether or not shitake mushrooms go well in a salad.

Even today's male movie stars are a distinctly androgynous lot, in no way akin to the manly likes of John Wayne or Kirk Douglas or Robert Mitchum. Meanwhile women on screen are trading punches with men, flinging them out windows, and bash-ing their faces to a pulp—amazingly, despite a seventy or eighty pound weight disadvantage. It's like a bantamweight kicking ass against Mike Tyson in his prime.

The nadir may have been when Hollywood tried to foist off Demi Moore as a Navy SEAL, even down to the crew cut. Demi was made to go through all manner of terrifying ordeals: harassed by sadistic officers, jeered at by dull-witted grunts, though of course she was a better warrior and even more foul-mouthed than any man. ("Suck my dick!" she at one point yells at a senior officer.) But of course not one second in the film was even remotely true. When poor Demi tried to act tough, I was reminded of that old movie where Bob Hope swaggered into a bar and ordered a lemonade.

Of course, for quite a while now the pea brains in Hollywood have been in the business of "empowering" women and raising their self-esteem, as if it were not grotesquely inflated already. No matter how ludicrously implausible, women have to be depicted as tougher than men. Though poor Demi was made to look like a man and talk like a man, she wasn't a man, and most definitely not a SEAL.

The extraordinary thing is that in almost every aspect of real life today, people are expected to take the feminist cartoon strip of reality for the real thing. It's one thing when female tennis players gripe about unequal pay when the men are not only better players, play five sets rather than three, and draw vastly larger crowds and TV viewership. Their double standard puts only logic at risk, not human lives.

But all across America today, fire departments and police stations have been compelled by the courts to hire the requisite number of women, physical standards be damned.

And in terms of real-world consequences, arguably the military is even worse. Having for years meekly taken their marching orders from the gender bullies, the top brass have changed everything from basic training on down to such a degree that men are demoralized by not being pushed enough. Pull-ups, forced marches with rifle and backpack have been all but eliminated; in their place came pursuits in which physically helpless women are bound to do better, like map reading, orientation, and so on. All this as the military heedlessly introduces more "gender friendly" equipment, like lighter but easier to carry rifles, and lighter hand grenades so the little women can avoid blowing themselves up.

Meanwhile, the top brass—themselves promoted at the behest of "progressive" politicians—boast of their enlightened attitude.

We should have learned the consequences of diminished standards back in 1994, with the tragic case of Kara Hultgreen, but of course we did not. Piloting a $38 million F-14A Tomcat fighter off the USS *Abraham Lincoln*, Lt. Hultgreen wound up dead at the bottom of the sea. A subsequent investigation revealed she had absolutely no business being in the cockpit. During her training, Lt. Hultgreen had received consistently low scores, including "four downs" (major errors). For a man, one or two "downs" are enough to be discharged.

Worse, she had failed the test involving landing on flattops. But so intimidated were our military by the leading Congressional harridans of the day, chiefly Pat Schroeder and Barbara Boxer, that they went out of their way to recruit women, suitability be damned.

Needless to say, the feminist politicians went on to cushy retirements without ever questioning their choices or their agenda.

Meanwhile, back in Hollywood, women continue to pummel men with abandon, teaching the Kara Hultgreens of the world exactly the wrong lesson.

I say bring back Bette Davis, Barbara Stanwyck, and Ava Gardner—women who knew a lot about empowerment and sending men reeling, without having to use their fists.

TEN

More Fun with Feminists

American daytime television couldn't get enough of me. I also did *Oprah*. Twice.

The first time went well. Before going on the air, Oprah asked me what I thought of black women, adding that her viewing audience—which I was led to understand would be fifty percent African-American—"will be very interested in that." They are great company, I said, enthusiastically, emphasizing the adjective so that no one could miss my meaning, then elaborating with language that was a little more spicy and even more specific. When I later added that my ideal woman was the proverbial whore in the bedroom, cook in the kitchen, and lady in the drawing room, Oprah and some girls in the studio audience actually began cheering. I was her hero of 1982.

Five years later, not so much.

The theme this time was older men who date younger women.

Perfect. At my suggestion, a good friend of mine was also included, and the show flew us both to Chicago from New York. My buddy was a highly decorated Special Forces hero in Vietnam—two silver stars—named Chuck Pfeifer. Captain Pfeifer was the straightest of straight shooters. When Oprah asked right up front why we preferred younger women, I chickened out and said that younger women were more likely to put up with silly pursuits such as night-clubbing and heavy drinking, whereas older women, being more mature, would never allow it. The mostly female audience seemed to like that. But then Captain Pfeifer got into action. "Only a blind man would prefer an older woman," bellowed the good captain, and the hissing drowned out the rest of his philippic.

While figuratively dodging rotten vegetables, I tried my best to recover some ground. I evoked the Don Giovanni syndrome—men thinking they'll find happiness through variety. But it was too late. We'd lost the hostess, and her audience followed, and we were good-naturedly booed off the stage, and probably off television forever.

The final nail in our coffin was that the only males in the audience, three black men, stood up and agreed with us, which clearly offended Oprah even more. Indeed, they managed to get us into trouble through association by expanding on the general theme, explaining that their own preference for younger women was partly based on older women . . . smelling bad.

In other words, in today's parlance, "they spoke their truth," as well as the universal one that men find younger women more attractive than older ones.

This, of course, should not be controversial. It is simple fact and always has been. Even the great King Solomon, seeking a woman for a new wife, had his acolytes bring forth fifty or more females they deemed suitable for him: wise ones, smart ones, some who had the right build for child-bearing, tall ones, gentle ones, serious ones. And the wise king looked them over until his eye suddenly caught sight of, on the far edge of the crowd of candidates, a cutie-pie with a dimple on her ear, and that was that!

So, again, nothing we said on Oprah's program should have aroused the least indignation, let alone fury. That it did is a lamentable fact of the times, for women have been well tutored in the performative anger born of . . . what, exactly?

Hippocrates, the father of Western medicine, would have said envy. During the Periclean period, around 430 BC, he discovered and named a disease known as "micropoulaki." He did not call it a virus, but a sickness of the brain. Some years later, Aristotle described micropoulaki syndrome as a disease, but one that is not contagious, "any more than a fool can influence an intelligent fellow to act foolishly." In classical Greek, micropoulaki translates as having a tiny willy, so women should, by definition, be immune from the disease. But strange as it may seem, thanks to feminism they are now known to suffer from it. The symptoms are terrible: feverish envy, raging periods of jealousy, hysterical fulminations, foaming at the mouth, howling at the moon, blustering, and so on. Also, inventing facts while denying others.

The irony of this sickness is that although man has invented the printing press, conquered various deadly diseases, dreamed up the bikini, flown to the moon and back, and crossed the oceans underwater, he has not made a scintilla of progress against micropoulaki. It's as bad today, perhaps worse, as it was when Hippocrates first diagnosed it in Athens.

The bottom line is that we need a lot more truth telling between the sexes, not less.

But, of course, dummkopf feminists are chiefly in the business of denying truth, and by the millions women who once would have known better have heedlessly followed their lead.

How did this happen? How have the small-time Stalins and Maos of our day come to have the right and authority to tell the rest of us how to think and behave? I like being a sinner as much as I love my freedom, and these common people are getting in my way.

The answer goes right back to biology. There may be rationalizations aplenty, but the bottom line is that men have surrendered en masse for the simple reason that they will do literally anything to placate and please the fairer sex, with the ultimate goal of getting them between the sheets. Indeed, it can be called, in its convoluted way, rational behavior.

In many ways women can be said to be as smart as men, if not smarter. They are certainly more attuned to detail and to emotional nuance. Who would argue with that? (Even feminists will always accept the good parts.) And lots of them also have plenty of brain power by traditional measures, so justly earn success in fields of science and technology, that leave the poor little Greek boy hopelessly adrift.

But as a rule, women are simply not as rational as men.

Moreover, as everyone also knows, by nature women prefer the safety of the group over the risks of individuality. Which is to say—see the average audience on American daytime television—women are far more easily led.

Of course, a case can also be easily made that some of the more notable women these days really are just stupid.

And this, too, has a scientific basis. The oldest human fossil was a small-brained female by the name of Lucy, known as Australopithecus afarensis, who existed between 3.85 and 2.95 million years ago. And some would have it that human evolution followed a direct path from Lucy to modern woman. Kim Kardashian, for example, is a direct descendant of Lucy. So, too, beyond question, are members of the #MeToo movement. Their brains, like Kim's, have unaccountably remained as small, if not smaller, than Lucy's.

This puzzles paleoanthropologists, and frankly it also baffles yours truly. How can some women be lightning quick to seize any opportunity to get publicity and money, yet possess such tiny brains? Some scientists speculate that the bigger the breasts, the smaller the brain, but this theory has been disproved time and again, notably in experiments conducted in the Groucho Marx–Bob Hope institute of human evolution. American feminists are disputing these findings, but then they would, wouldn't they?

And yet, they prove it anew daily by their own behavior.

The power of feminism to alter life for the worse has shown itself in innumerable ways, as it distorts everything it touches. One of the most tragic of those ways, in my eyes, is its impact on fashion. For a woman who dresses badly lacks femininity, and lacking femininity she cannot possibly be beautiful in the true and classical sense of the word. I'm talking here primarily of the latter-day preference for trousers over skirts. Radical feminism does not accept a difference between the sexes, ergo the rage for unisex. But the right skirt instantly conveys more about a woman than any passport or CV.

There is absolutely no reason why women should look like men. The essential differences should be accentuated rather than diluted. But try to convince our modern dress designers of this. The fact that most successful couturiers are homosexuals might of course have something to do with it. In any case, their models generally look more like boys without bosoms and, worse yet, without bottoms. It is enough to drive one back to ancient Greek times!

As a Greek, I grew up believing in a different kind of feminism, one that celebrates female autonomy and beauty; and the female body, of which the most important part of all are the legs. Now everything has changed. Whereas sexual revolutionaries once demanded freedom, now they clamor for absolute control. Hence the uniform of the trousers.

The most ludicrous charge of all is that a skirt is responsible for sexual harassment. This is like saying wealth is responsible for crime—which I'm sure a lot of them believe also. As a matter of fact, there is far less date rape in societies that indulge in nudity, places like Italy, Spain, and Greece, and which likewise do not stigmatize the wolf whistle, than in Anglo-Saxon societies. It all has to do with acceptance of the important and inviolate differences between the sexes.

Arguably the most intelligent American woman ever was the beautiful Clare Boothe Luce, and I defy you to find a photograph of her in slacks. And of course, that single difference from today's feminists bespeaks countless others.

It is hardly that Mrs. Luce was a shrinking violet. Quite the contrary, she was a highly successful playwright and editor and a member of Congress before being named Eisenhower's ambassador to Italy. In the latter role, in 1953 she analyzed the Trieste problem between Tito and the Italian government in a manner that left the chauvinistic Italians, as well as Eisenhower and Dulles, open-mouthed with admiration.

But she never for a moment was less than feminine. Indeed, in the wake of the reception following this diplomatic triumph, she blurted out: "I could have said all this in a few words rather than the 480-page analysis I have just presented you with. All men are idiots. After all, women are not interested in sex. All they want is babies and security from men. Men are just too stupid to know it."

In short, notwithstanding all her accomplishments, her greatest achievement may have been the steadfastness of her standing up for biological reality. Always, unhesitatingly, she was ready to declare that her greatest achievement was that of wife and mother.

Eat your heart out feminism!

But there it was in a nutshell. And what's more, in her heart of hearts, most every woman knows it—knows, that is, that the noblest role of all is that of the mother and booster of the male ego.

Moreover, they know that the sex drives of the sexes, while highly complementary, are radically different, which makes sexual loyalty as powerful and omnipresent a female yearning as is the impulse to stray in the male. Obviously a double standard applies here, as it must for the institution of family and society itself to survive. The Germans classify perfect love as being "romantically" in love with one woman, "intellectually" in love with another, and "domestically" in love with one's wife. Theoretically (at least for a time), one may delude oneself that the object of one's adoration possesses all three; but that is a fine madness, indeed.

Here's what the brilliant Wall Street investor Paul Tudor Jones had to say on the subject not long ago in a speech at UVA: "You will never see as many great women investors or traders as men—end of story. As soon as that baby's lips touch the mother's bosom, forget it. Every single investment idea, every desire to understand what is going to make this go up or down is going to be overwhelmed by the most beautiful experience which a man will never share—a mode of connection between that mother and that baby."

I can't think of truer or more beautiful and tender words, yet when the *Washington Post* reported it, the usual sob sisters were immediately up in arms, and to his eternal disgrace, Paul apologized. Apologized for what? Silly question. One almost always needs to apologize for truth-telling these days, and to seek counseling as if caught red-handed committing a crime.

Yet most mothers I know indeed prefer their children to the stock ticker and its equivalent in other realms, whereas men would rush to choose the latter. The hairy contingent surely know this deep down, among myriad other things, but pretend not to know.

Needless to say, feminism has badly deformed politics in the land of the depraved, and by now the change is nothing short of intolerable. Although I love women more than life itself, excepting of course ardent feminists, their judgment is not to be trusted, they are staggeringly ill informed and they are followers. They reflexively champion the expansion of government more than men do, and the welfare system bribes them to have nothing to do with the men who impregnate them. Socialism has turned them by the millions into wards of the state, and no-fault divorce ensures they become dependent on handouts rather than on men. Moreover, government mandates now ensure that they get jobs ahead of men, qualifications be damned, and the explosion of government jobs is among their most frequent source of employment.

In other words, the feminist-inspired policies of the left have succeeded in further turning women against men, even as they have simultaneously also turned them into wards of the state.

The truth is, women are instinctively drawn toward the idea of a polity as kindergarten. They hate competitiveness, vigorous debate, risk-taking. Better to leave everything to the nice teacher.

Once again, I am forced to conclude that the so-called reactionaries who fought tooth and nail against giving the weaker sex the vote had a point. It was a terrible idea, and we are all suffering the consequences.

With all of this, by the way, I have little doubt Mrs. Luce would agree.

For feminists, sex is and must be a battle, one as desperate and fraught with consequence as Thermopylae. But actually it is, or should be, more of a piano duet, with no aggressor stroking the keys. Indeed, in the great scheme of things, the sex act itself is a much more casual and unimportant thing than it is customarily admitted to be, at least for those who have ready access to it. Those perpetually aggrieved on the subject seem to me like that crazy Rochester wife up in the attic, only this time they're often in soulless newsrooms in DC, New York, and London.

Instead of being able to comment in a lighthearted way about matters sexual, their reflex is instant outrage.

This is so—and perhaps even more so—when the offender is of their own sex. One lady who got in hot water for speaking the truth was a certain Princeton grad named Sue Patton, who wrote a letter to her Ivy League sisters urging them to put their college years to good use and find a hubby. She would have got off more lightly if she had announced that Adolf Hitler was great in the sack. Never have I heard such epithets hurled at a lady. A traitor to feminism! When all Patton had done was acknowledge a truth that a few generations past was common understanding.

Back when a principal function of schools for smart women was enabling them to pair off with smart men, both sexes were well served by the arrangement. For contrary to feminist dogma, and after all the fun and games, men want intellectually equal companions.

Through it all, that pesky thing, reality, keeps poking through.

According to surveys, American women have even discovered that men want casual sex more than they do. There are also reports that for some women sex remains much less enjoyable than it is for men. Hold the presses! Yet in committed relationships, women report wanting sex as often as men do. *Gott im Himmel!* And yet more earth-shattering discoveries by American women: The acts American girls are engaging in, from oral sex to sexting, tend to be staged for boys' enjoyment.

Indeed, many American girls say that after they've had sex or administered oral sex to boys, they've had little satisfaction and sense that the boys have been in charge. Duhhhhh! American women who research such matters now write that "it's hard for me to consider a penis in my mouth as impersonal." I imagine so, although I've never had one in my mouth. These same women also write that "it's pornography which teaches boys to expect constantly willing, fully waxed girls to imitate all those arched backs and movie-perfect moans." Well, I don't watch porn a lot—in fact, almost never—but I do expect an arched back once in a while.

Of course, this is all news to modern feminists, who believe they've invented the wheel. In fact, in the most vital ways girls have never changed. They have always felt guilty after giving a blowjob, but grateful they didn't have to go all the way. Alcohol has always played a big part in seduction. Boys have always been more judgmental after sex than girls. That's because they had an orgasm and the girls didn't. Next time, just ask Taki.

We need more of this—more honesty that is, not more blowjobs.

American women need to focus more on women's nature, which is always of a finer texture. To concentrate on women's courage and women's strengths. And to stop complaining and stop reading history for the sole purpose of proving that men are and have always been shits.

And for good measure, if they insist on reading someone the riot act, they should head for Saudi Arabia and read it to them. They need it more than we do.

The #MeToo movement is of course the natural consequence of the feminists' now fifty-plus years of ugly work. Those men not in retreat are in a permanent crouch. It's no surprise that so many of them are depressed and overweight these days; living with such women takes its toll.

Having been too feminized by the constant #MeToo propaganda to be able to hold firm, they actually root for movie superheroes to defeat super monsters. The whole nation has been dumbed down to moronic levels.

Thanks to #MeToo, what used to be called getting railroaded is now called justice. It happens to the ordinary and famous alike.

Mia Farrow fostered a Medea-like revenge against Woody Allen, as good an artist as there is nowadays, because he'd dropped her in favor of the young South Korean she'd adopted. And though the charges against Woody had twice been investigated and dismissed, the cancel culture prevailed and killed his career. Even his memoir was shelved. How dare he publish something that the Farrows, Ronan and Dylan, as well as their hideous mother, didn't agree with? The trio would have fitted in nicely back in 1930s Berlin.

Cowardice is certainly not new, especially in movies and publishing, but for all the continued wailing and gnashing of teeth about the blacklist of the Fifties, what we're seeing now is something of an entirely different order.

America has turned into a bad joke, a paradise for phonies, self-important grievance-mongers, foul-mouthed whiny women, vomit-inducing feminists, and *New York Times* imbeciles.

A bell needs to be sounded to wake us all up about what is happening. The phonies have taken over and are using strong-arm tactics to silence anyone they don't agree with. They want to remake man and society in their own image. Well, it is time we stood up and told them to shove it.

These hate-mongers are out to do away with our past, calling it a mythology while spreading misinformation and lies about it. We've had a glorious past and men have played the greater part in it because that is how God meant it to be.

Today's clowns are against nature and they will not, cannot, win.

One can only hope that in the end, real women will not allow it.

ELEVEN

How to Be a Man? Ask the Expert!

"HOW TO BE A MAN" was, in fact, the title that appeared not long ago atop a *Spectator* column of mine. But it is far more than that. It is the question I have asked, and sought to answer, all of my life.

When I wrote the piece in question, I had just been visited at my home in the Alps by a Dutch TV crew of five who were filming a program with exactly that title. It was to star a single person, me. Their thinking, more like a flattering presumption, was that the little Greek boy had all the answers.

Either that, or that I would be the butt of the joke.

This is what the mother of my children strongly suspected. She warned that the people from Dutch national television would do a hatchet job to top all hatchet jobs on me. Point well-taken. The Western mainstream media is dead set against traditional manhood, and pretty much everything else that speaks to a better time. It talks nonstop about justice and compassion and fairness, while encouraging envy, repression, and revenge.

If I had my way there would be a total boycott of the media, a massive cancellation of cable television services, and the creation of an alternative social media system.

But although I don't have my way, I still have my opinions, and in this case I convinced myself I actually didn't give a damn and would take the leap. Even if it came to the worst, between their edits I'd get out at least some of what I believe about this age of lunatic feminists and prime-time hate-mongers posing as utopians, and how today's youth is shell-shocked from being bombarded with nothing but lies about young men, unless they're members of the LGBTQ community—what the hell does the Q stand for? In short, how we are accused of being part of a rape culture merely for being men, because admiring a woman these days is tantamount to being a leering rapist, opening a door for a lady is no longer gentlemanly but the act of a Neanderthal. Hollywood films are not helping, nor is what passes today as literature. Tomes on the history of manhood and all its supposed crimes fill bookstore windows, more than a few by traitors to their sex in which men confess to horrors.

So I'd say all that, or at least as much as I could squeeze in. And maybe mention Spengler's famous observation about how an individual's life cycle and a civilization's were the same: childhood, youth, manhood, and old age—noting that our civilization now shows signs of being post-senile. I'd say that in fact our past was glorious, and that it was men who had played the greater part in it, because that is how God meant it to be.

No matter what, I'd at least get in some licks.

My questioner, one Margriet van der Linden, proved to be a statuesque Viking-like blonde, and she indeed did put me through the ringer. We spent three days talking about manhood in the age of #MeToo, and rarely have I been asked so many challenging questions.

Not incidentally (for it had bearing on the matters at hand), I took breaks during the filming to mix it up in karate training with my sensei Richard Amos. Richard had been regularly putting me through my paces—karate, gym with weights, cross-country skiing, a downhill or two when the sun was out—so the TV crew came to the dojo, where my sensei and I gave them a bit of a show kicking and punching each other, and otherwise showing what it's all about. Which is that implicit in karate is a sense of personal dignity, and that for some of us the way of Bushido, once characteristic of the samurai, remains a code of moral principle.

I had been hooked since the evening in 1966 when I first discovered karate at the Palais de Sport in Cannes, and I have yet to miss a day of practice since, except when out with injuries.

Aside from being as brainy as any karate teacher around, Richard Amos is as tough on the floor as they come. His timing and focus are such that it's almost impossible to land a solid hit. Margriet was impressed, I could tell, and she asked him some intelligent questions.

Naturally, some of the taped conversation that followed had to do with sport. I may be a small-timer where sport is concerned, I told her, but one thing I've never done is quit, whether competing in tennis, karate, judo, even polo. I said that when I won the judo world championship in Brussels 2008 in the category for seventy-year-olds and over, my coach told me just before the final: "You're a bum and fighting another bum. So if you lose, find your own way home—I don't want to have anything to do with you."

Talk about putting pressure on the poor little Greek boy.

But it worked. It has to do with personal dignity, and manhood, and it was the toughest kind of tough love.

Even now, after sixty years of training experience, I cannot accept that my karate life will no longer be filled with new possibilities. Getting stronger and faster, kicking higher, were the old goals. Now I seek to move more effortlessly and look better aesthetically. The irony of this is that the more one loses one's self in the inner unseen workings, the better the technique becomes on the surface.

So we spoke quite a while about sport. I noted how part of the experience of sport at the top level resides in dealing with the finality of it. It is win or lose, and that's the end of it, so it can often feel like a kind of death. This is not true of almost anything else in life until the real thing. (Finish a great book and one can always read it again.) Moreover, the pursuit of excellence, combined with the need for courage and personal discipline, make sport unique—or, as I added, at least that was once the case. Now that most sports are simply entertainment, that ethos of sport is long gone.

How is that particular to being a man? How do the sexes differ in the sporting realm? Simple—in most sport the levels of achievement are dramatically different. Men are stronger, faster, better. If you want equal pay, you compete equally, said yours truly: best of five sets, men and women in the same draw. That's equality, as in equestrian events. And for brainless TV pundits who inform us that gender is fluid and not determined at birth, none of this pretending men are women.

In short, the Dutch just put out their nets and I swam into them.

The lady interviewer was very skilled at her work. Taking me through my life story, it was obvious she had read *The Spectator* columns with evangelical zeal because she knew all about me. When she put it to me bluntly—"What has happened to men?"—my short answer was: #MeToo.

And, I must say, though I do not speak Dutch and don't know anyone who does, I believe in the end they were very fair. My part was in English and they didn't touch it up or add any American feminist-type rubbish. If it had been an American crew, I'd probably be on Rikers.

I even got into how these brainless American female hustlers today challenge men's great literary achievements. For example, a female clown critic wrote that Zelda Fitzgerald's madness was because her husband Scott cribbed from her. Imagine: The great Scott, author of *The Great Gatsby* and *Tender Is the Night* among other heartrending novels, cribbed from the poor, tragic, mad-as-a-hatter Zelda. Talk about true madness! She may have been a good writer on occasion, but she wasn't anywhere near him.

And—need it even be said?—my other great literary hero, Hemingway, has fared far worse. Sportsmanship, manhood, gallantry, even heterosexuality are out, so naturally so is Papa. (And let's not even mention Christianity.) No one ever wrote more beautifully about the active life, the tranquil exhilaration of fishing, but also about the brutality of big-game hunting, bullfighting, and war. His masculine prose had the effect of the utmost subtlety. It was the hardest way to write because it seemed so easy and natural.

When Hemingway did himself in, the newspapers falsely reported it as an accident. In fact, unable to live up to his title as the world's literary heavyweight champion (in Norman Mailer's characterization) Papa went out with a bang, like a champ. He'd been in the wars too long and despite the mess, it was a graceful exit. An overdose would have been very un-Hemingwayesque.

I remember reading about it the next day in my Aunt Sophia's garden in Athens like it was yesterday, and I decided right then and there that the writing life was the one for me.

This is the giant today's literary types speak of as non-literary and vulgar.

I readily allowed to the interviewer that while a man needn't be dominant, or at least not make a show of his dominance, he needs to have a spine, and be willing to speak the truth about who he fundamentally is—even if doing so nowadays means having to take on the entire drift of the culture. Needless to say, it's impossible to avoid today's sniveling moral arbiters, who appear not only on television but in elite media like the *New York Times* and *The New Yorker*. The women tastemakers are shrieking harridans, and the men moral dullards akin to queasy teenagers squeezing their pimples who weep watching Harry and Meghan on the tube. To these, what passes as a man of good sense and taste is someone lacking any originality and the courage to defend what is best in their civilization, even in the unlikely event they recognize what it is.

So I had my full say, which may be summed up as: God save us from the never-ending bullshit of #MeToo!

One hopes that at least a few Dutch TV viewers may have been enlightened.

Taki outside London's Royal Courts of Justice, defending a libel case, 1986.

Taki and Alexandra with their two children,
Mandolyna and John-Taki,
at home in Gstaad, 2010.

Taki at age twenty-one, with Joan Collins at El Morocco nightclub, New York, 1957.

PARIS
MATCH
N° 638/1er JUILLET 1961/0,80 NF
c'est
une « deb »...
la mode anglaise
de « l'entrée dans le monde »
passe la Manche
Deux cents débutantes françaises
(dont celle-ci,
Christina de Caraman)
ont leur premier bal
à Versailles

Left: Taki's first wife Cristina de Caraman, daughter of the Duke de Caraman, as Deb of the Year, cover of *Paris Match*, 1962.

Above: Taki's wife Princess Alexandra Schoenburg-Hartenstein, *Vogue*, 1967.

Top: Alexandra and Taki at Maxim's, Paris, 1972.

Above left: Brigitte Bardot and Taki at a Saint-Tropez nightclub, 1968.

Above right: Unknown girl picked up off the Greek coast for a ride on the first *Bushido*, 1970.

Top: Demonstrating a flying karate kick for the idle rich aboard *Atlantis*, 1975.

Above: As captain of the team leading Greece to the European Championships in Zurich, 1976.

Left: Belgrade, 1978.

PROUST QUESTIONNAIRE

My greatest extravagances: "Yachts, chalets, mistresses, and gambling."

TAKI

Now in his fourth decade as a columnist for *The Spectator,* in London, the ageless international Lothario, critic, and Renaissance man reminisces about a life plucked from fiction

What is your idea of perfect happiness?
Winning gold in the Olympics for Greece; having Keira Knightley fall in love with me; writing *A Moveable Feast;* and watching my two kids playing with my two grandchildren in the garden of my Swiss chalet—and not dropping dead à la *The Godfather.*

Which living person do you most admire?
The Unknown Soldier.

What is the trait you most deplore in yourself?
Wanting to be liked.

What is your greatest fear?
Losing face—chickening out in public.

What is the trait you most deplore in others?
Bootlicking upward, kicking downward.

What do you consider the most overrated virtue?
Oozing charm.

What is your greatest extravagance?
Yachts, chalets, mistresses, and gambling.

On what occasion do you lie?
Only in order not to wound . . . and, of course, when trying to seduce a woman.

What is your most marked characteristic?
Not taking anything too seriously.

What is it that you most dislike?
Snobbishness.

What is the quality you most like in a man?
Courage—both physical and moral.

What is the quality you most like in a woman?
Femininity.

Which words or phrases do you most overuse?
"With all due respect, you're full of shit."

Which living person do you most despise?
Robert Mugabe.

Which historical figure do you most identify with?
Robert E. Lee.

What or who is the greatest love of your life?
My wife, Alexandra, by far.

When and where were you happiest?
When I landed my *Spectator* column 33 years ago.

What do you consider your greatest achievement?
Perhaps having been of a happy disposition throughout my life.

What is your most treasured possession?
My library of close to 10,000 books, and a few good paintings.

Who is your favorite hero of fiction?
Dick Diver, from *Tender Is the Night.*

What is your greatest regret?
Having wasted the little talent I possess.

How would you like to die?
Giving up the last seat in the last lifeboat of a sinking liner to a young beautiful girl, and returning to the first-class lounge for a final drink. 

"Mr Taki, Stacey Keach, George Best—I'm sorry mate, but you want the executive cells!"

Sir Denis Thatcher Bt.
36 CHESHAM PLACE
LONDON SW1X 8HB

TELEPHONE 0171 235 6600
FAX 0171 259 5366

29th August 2000

Dear Taki,

I have made many many visits all over the world over many years but never one as the days we spent in Gstaad. I do not know how to express my thanks. Your hospitality in the hotel was overwhelming.

Through your care and thoughtfulness we had a whole series of lunches and dinners and met so many charming and generous people.

Above all else it was you who made the days. Your kindness of the perfect host, your attention to every detail and the friendship you bestowed on us was such that I will remember "our little Greek boy" for many a year.

Thank you too for your parting gift, so typical of your generosity.

With thanks and regards to you both.

Yours ever, Denis

Taki Theodoracopoulos

Top left: A Davis Cup victory, 1967.

Top right: A cartoon from *The Standard*, December 1984.

Above: A thank you note from Sir Denis Thatcher, 2000.

Opposite page: *Vanity Fair*, May 2010.

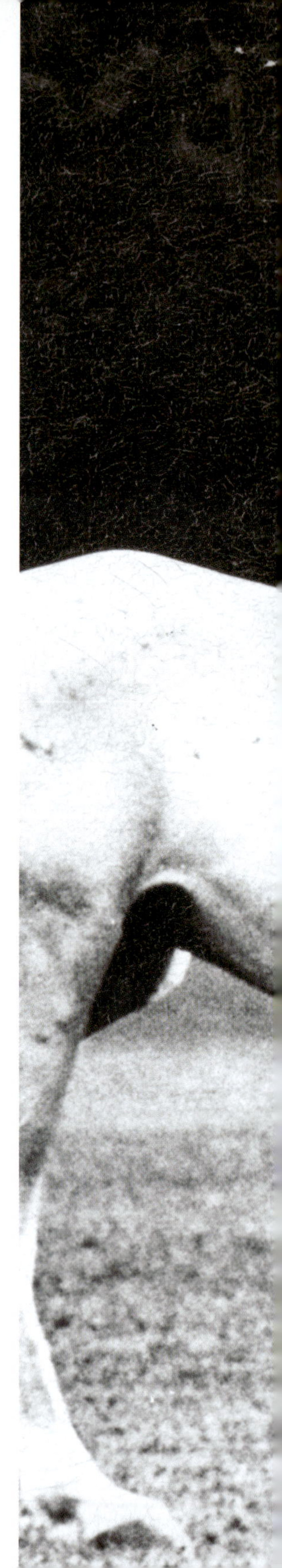

Above and right: Winning a polo match in Parc de Bagatelle, Paris, 1970.

Top: Taki and Alexandra at their wedding, 1981.

Above: Alexandra with best men, famed editor and mentor Clay Felker and Christopher Buckley, writer and son of William F. Buckley Jr.

Above: Taki and Alexandra relaxing after skiing
at the Eagle Club, Gstaad, 2006.

KENSINGTON PALACE

September: 7th
1996.

Dear Taki,

What a wonderful evening you gave us on Friday!
It was lovely to be with you, Cosi, Charlie & Tyler!
How impressed I was by your profound knowledge of my fairer sex & consequently came to the conclusion thats its all because you're a Greek!

Thank you so much, Taki, for inviting me to dinner, as I was very touched to be thought of...

With love from,

Diana.

Taki,

Wishing you a very Happy Christmas
and New Year
1996

With love from,

Diana.

KENSINGTON PALACE

May: 11th
1997.

Dearest Taki,

Thank you for the support & understanding you constantly show in your Sunday column - I'm enormously touched & did so much want you to know that....
Friends, in the media, can be hard to find, but your friendship is treasured & immensely appreciated.

Lots of love from, Diana x

This page: A holiday card and notes from Princess Diana thanking Taki for the various dinners he hosted to introduce her to friends in the press, 1996 and 1997.

Opposite page: A letter from President Richard Nixon, 1985.

RICHARD NIXON

January 23, 1985

26 FEDERAL PLAZA
NEW YORK CITY

Dear Taki,

I was distressed to learn of some of your current problems and wanted to send you a word of encouragement.

Since the time Bob Tyrrell introduced us a few years ago, I have been one of your admirers. You are a rare bird - an intellectual who sees the world as it really is rather than just as he wants it to be. That is why your foreign policy columns have always made such eminent good sense.

In the years immediately ahead when great changes will take place in the world scene, your voice needs to be heard. That is why I profoundly hope that you will recover completely from the problems which led to your present difficulties and will be able to devote your extraordinary talents full time to the cause of creating better understanding of the great issues confronting the world.

I hope we meet at some time in the future under better circumstances.

Sincerely,

RN

Mr. Taki Theodoracopulos

My mother was as Spartan as they come. Among the other things I remember her telling me about were the institutions of Spartan government—aristocratic and orienting the citizens toward the ideals of a warrior life. *I tan I epi tas*—with it or on it—was the message every Spartan mother gave her son as he left to wage war. With your shield as a victor, or on it as a corpse.

Today this sounds so drastic, female pundits would be demanding jail for such mothers. So too does the Spartan custom of younger men borrowing older men's wives to give them children and produce strong warriors. (The English upper classes still more or less follow this practice—it was one of the reasons I moved to Britain back in the swinging Sixties.) But it helped a tiny martial state defeat the barbarians and eventually win a catastrophic war against Athens, the greatest cultural state ever. Needless to say, Spartan kings were the first in the line of battle, unflinchingly eager to show their troops how to die. And the men were ready learners. Archers and javelin throwers, who launched from afar, were not held in the same esteem as those who fought at great risk to themselves. Sword and spear were likewise highly regarded, the rest was looked upon with suspicion.

Long ago as those events occurred, their spirit survives in my homeland. I was brought up learning about honor-obsessed men, paragons of male strength, courage, endurance, and patrician manners.

Greeks have always stressed honor as the cardinal virtue—to be manifest not just in warfare, but in every aspect of a man's life, very much including—make that especially—in his treatment of women. For it is precisely because nature has endowed men with not only greater size and strength, but with the biological imperative to pursue the opposite sex, that the rules have been designed to protect the fairer sex.

Desirable as she might be, a woman is never to be treated with anything less than courtesy and respect.

TWELVE

Honor—The First Manly Virtue

It was from my Spartan mother, when I was ver
that I first heard about Leonidas and his response w
Persians offered safe passage and great riches if the
would lay down their arms. "Molon labe" was his disd
ply—"Come and get them."

Those two little words spoken in 480 BC remain am
most noble ever uttered, bestowing immortality on L
and his 300 for their preference of death over a life of co
and shame. When the Persians tried to reason with the S
by telling them their million arrows would hide the s
nidas responded that this was excellent news, since th
fight in the shade. Gallows humor perhaps, but deeply f
Spartans thought arrows mere spindles, to be swiped av
their shields.

In Homer, bravery was the hallmark of nobles, heroes, and demigods like Achilles, but so too were high-mindedness and rectitude. Ruthless as they were in battle, they were scrupulous in their personal honor. Pericles was the model, his idealistic patriotism free from all sordid and selfish motives marking him as the greatest statesman ever. But the list of the men I'd like to have known is endless: Cimon of Athens, Miltiades, Themistocles, Pheidias, Praxiteles, Socrates, Plato, Aristides, Sophocles, Aeschylus, Euripides, Aristophanes, Plutarch, Thucydides, Hippocrates—you name them, we Greeks had them.

Indeed, the Greeks not only invented modern warfare, a collision of soldiers on an open plain where courage and physical prowess were paramount, but fair play on the battlefield, and the protection of women and noncombatants.

My mother died at ninety-two. She was the youngest of thirteen. Some had died in war, others in bed, but all had lived honorably. None were idle, all led useful lives. When I was a young boy, she used to take me to see the Greek boys leaving for the front, where her four brothers and her husband already were. She never once showed fear during the war and the bloody communist uprising of 1944. Later, she worried nonstop about my drinking and prayed daily I would not have a car crash. Yet, she cheerfully encouraged me as a reporter to go to Vietnam and the Middle East in wartime.

In my own small way I've tried to live up to my forebears by never backing off, and by hero-worshipping the defenders of Iwo Jima, and the US Marine Corps among many others, including the Polish lancers' charge at Somosierra (successful) and that of Pickett (unsuccessful) at Gettysburg.

What kind of person is willing to sacrifice his life for an ideal?

One of my great heroes is Major Axel von dem Bussche, one of the few plotters in the failed attempt by patriotic German officers to kill Hitler who survived. From an old aristocratic Saxon family, his regiment, the 9th Infantry, was an elitist and patrician body comparable to Britain's Brigade of Guards. More members of the resistance came from the 9th than any other Wehrmacht regiment; nineteen were executed after July 20. Ironically, it was his very skill and courage in the 1940 campaign that first put Axel, one of the regiment's standouts, in a position to kill Hitler when he volunteered at twenty-four to "model" a new army coat before the Fuhrer. Selected for his battlefield exploits, his plan was to detonate the grenades inside the pockets. But Hitler canceled the demonstration at the last minute. So Axel screwed up his courage twice.

What made him do it? In the attack against Leningrad, he had been badly wounded, shot through the lung—he was later to lose his leg—and while recuperating he saw the terrible reprisals the Germans were committing against the Ukrainians. That was all and it was enough. It was then and there that he decided Hitler must be stopped.

Or maybe it was the genes. Incredibly, his first cousin, Anders Lassen, won the Victoria Cross fighting in the British Army, the only foreigner to do so in World War II.

Theodore Roosevelt was another of my heroes. Before the turn of the century, in the war against Spain, the committed patriot formed his own Rough Riders battalion and charged up San Juan Hill in Cuba to win the most celebrated battle of the war. No one who saw Teddy lead his riders up the hill under withering fire expected him to come back alive. But he did, and when the United States entered the European Great War in April 1917, T.R.—who had campaigned relentlessly for America's entry while his successor dissembled—went to see Wilson, demanding at age fifty-nine a combat role on the Western Front. Typically, Wilson saw only a political opponent, and did what he did best, dissemble, before turning him down. But if American boys were to die, T.R. wanted his own sons to fight, and all four of them did. Quentin was shot down and killed, and Archie and Teddy Jr. were badly wounded. The Second World War found the surviving three brothers, now pushing fifty, anxious for combat duty, and all three achieved it.

In fact, they tried as hard as possible for the most dangerous assignments in units where the other men were of an age to be their sons. Ted Jr. even sent his younger brother Kermit a white feather because he had not enlisted quite as fast as Ted felt he should have. Theodore Roosevelt Jr., age fifty-seven, went ashore with his son on D-Day, the oldest man in the invasion force. Walking with a cane, he personally led U.S. troops on Utah Beach, winning the Medal of Honor posthumously in an action General Bradley called the bravest he saw in wartime.

The leftist Brit journalist Anthony Howard once called the children of T.R., and others who volunteer in times of crisis, dumb. And it is undoubtably true that in like circumstances Howard would never have risked his own skin. But the men who answer the call to arms, and especially who volunteer for it, are not dumb. They are superior. They are men of honor.

Personally, the thing I'm proudest of in all my life is that on October 28, 1940, the day Italy invaded Greece, my mother had a husband and five brothers racing to the front.

Indeed, my own father provided an incomparable model of honorable behavior. So did my uncle, Nikita Varvitsiotis, a tall, proud Spartan MP known throughout his political career for standing up in parliament and in a booming voice charging left-wingers of being Bulgarians—in other words, traitors to the mother country. Not by any means a safe thing to do. But Nikita lived by the old virtues of bravery, patriotism, responsibility, and, most of all, honor.

Yet when Mussolini attacked Greece, Nikita was among the first in the fight against his former ally.

Once, at a party in New York, the talk turned to the Spanish Civil War, and in due course I said that my uncle and cousins had been volunteers in that bloody struggle. Instantly, one of the society ladies present approached me, arms open, saying, "Let me give you a hug." "Before you do," said I, "you should probably ask for which side."

As a child I met many soldiers who had returned home having had horrendous experiences, yet all I remember are the funny things they told me. For instance, my uncle told a wonderful tale of having been stabbed in his backside by a panicky Italian Alpini he had captured in the later fight for Crete. Drawing his pistol, he took away the Italian's stiletto, then forced him to dress the wound he had inflicted.

Of course, our family was hardly unique in this regard. Unlike the French and Dutch and other occupied peoples, during World War II, the Greeks never stopped fighting. Their high morale implied chivalry and humanity as well as courage. When the last Greek fort's line of supply was finally cut off, and they were forced to come out, the German commander mounted a guard of honor for them.

These days, needless to say, the concept of honor is everywhere in retreat. In no way is this more evident than in an arena with which I am all too familiar, that of sports. Indeed, in retrospect the precipitous decline in honorable behavior on the playing fields that began fifty and sixty years ago may be seen as a harbinger of the general societal collapse we see today.

My uncle competed in the hurdles in both the 1932 and 1936 Olympics, and my father was on the relay team. Back then, athletics were only for pure amateurs, and even on the professional level anyone caught violating high standards of conduct risked suspension or worse. Famously, the great Jim Thorpe was obliged to give back his Olympic track medal for having competed professionally in another sport. *Chariots of Fire* captured the will, luminosity, and purity of the amateur athlete who competes honorably for glory and would rather die than cheat.

Once, winning was not everything. It is recalled by tennis historians that in the final of the 1940 U.S. National Championships in Forest Hills, Don McNeill, believing his opponent's ball was unjustly being called out, threw point after point to Bobby Riggs, and still beat him in five sets. And the same was commonplace when I was on the circuit, players giving back points they believed they'd unjustly won over others.

It all went back to the chivalric code, and it lasted until the ghastly Sixties. 1968 was not just the worst year for Western civilization, it also took away the smiles of our tennis-playing children, who as always emulated their heroes. For on the circuit, smiling was suddenly out, sneering was in. I remember in earlier years practicing with the great Roy Emerson, and having to stop because he kept cracking me up.

Somehow, always laughing, Emmo won all those Grand Slams. But now it was as if being a gent meant being a loser.

Until very recently, sport was a great social leveler, in that players from humble backgrounds adhered to the protocol of the game established by the upper class. Tennis whites were de rigueur. The uniformity signified that the game was larger and more important than the individual. Good sportsmanship was also expected and enforced.

Players now give the umpire the finger. Instead of developing character, modern sport tends to forgive felonies. In America, universities serve as farm clubs for professional teams, where a star athlete can graduate from a top university while barely knowing how to read or write.

Even the handshake, universal symbol of goodwill and good sportsmanship, is under attack. A Simi Valley, California, high school actually banned it for fear the handshake might turn into a brawl after a sporting event. Some "athletes" were spitting on their hands before shaking. Others shook with one hand and punched with the other.

And all this is before we get to that other calamity of modern public life, displays of over-the-top emotion. When did the crying start? I've no idea. At least when Pete Sampras did it in the middle of a match he had a valid excuse, as his coach had just died of leukemia. But then the greatest of them all, Roger Federer, cried in Paris, and it's been downhill ever since. A crying jag in public would surely have embarrassed my old friend Baron von Cramm, a three-time losing Wimbledon finalist, not to mention Rod Laver, Roy Emerson, and John Newcombe, all three multiple winners of the crown. No one, not even the women, cried back then, especially in public. Angela Mortimer, Ann Jones, even Ginny Wade in the Jubilee Year, would not have dreamt of it.

As for myself, I will admit I blubbed a bit after I fought my last judo match. But I made sure no one witnessed that dishonorable event.

The only time before that was when I lost my first wrestling match, aged eleven, at boarding school, and even then it was a humiliation. Crying was supposed to be for sissies, but now sissies are in and tough guys are out. Can you imagine what it would have looked like if Jesse Owens had cried in front of Hitler?

When it comes to the fairer sex, playful and ardent as I've always been, never have I been anything but honorable in my conduct. I've always been keenly aware that being a gentleman means there are lines not to be crossed; that discretion is vital and reputations are not to be besmirched; that a "no" is to be accepted with good grace; that, above all, under any and all circumstances the weaker sex is to be physically protected.

Even as a callow youth, this last was always uppermost in my mind. I recall an episode that occurred in 1957, on the 7th of March to be precise. Though no longer in school, I'd continued my custom of crossing the ocean by ship, and on this occasion I was taking the *Liberté* from Le Havre to New York, along with my friends Leonidas Goulandris and John Zographos. Each of us had a suite, and entertained high hopes of romance on the high seas. The *Liberté* was truly a beauty, with the most wonderful paneling and grand salons, but what it lacked on that particular trip was women. There were eighty Venezuelan businessmen on board, and c'est tout.

Then Zographos went down to steerage and found a German girl who looked as if she hadn't had a bath since the Berlin blockade four years earlier. He upgraded her to first, took her to dinner in the private first-class dining room, where Goulandris was sick all over her. When she went to the lavatory to clean up, a drunken Venezuelan assaulted her, and though badly outnumbered, the three of us went to her rescue. At the time I had a broken leg, so I used my crutches against the South American brutes, bending one of my sticks against the hard head of the rapist.

Of course that's what we did. We would not have been able to face ourselves if we'd done otherwise. Nor would I say we were at all special in that regard; any group of well-brought-up young men would have done the same. It was how society, or rather the social order, worked back then.

I still bridle at the fact we were confined to quarters for the rest of the trip.

Mind you, one did not fight casually. Getting hit is not like in the movies. A proper punch if it lands breaks the jaw, knocks out teeth, and causes a concussion. A judo slam on the pavement can cause death if the head makes first contact.

But the honor code that then prevailed kept the skirmishing to the minimum. In all those years I only hit first once. It was in a Paris nightclub, over a girl, naturally, and I regret it still. I became a friend of the victim and apologized to him for close to fifty years, until his death, and I still feel ashamed.

Walking away is always the best policy; brave men do it all the time. Bullies are invariably cowards, so a strong threat, delivered with enough authority, is usually enough to do the trick.

Surprising as it seems, in my case this seems to be nearly as true at my current age as it was thirty and forty years ago. One afternoon not long ago I was standing outside my hotel in Cadogan Gardens, London, watching as a mother with two tiny children in the back was trying to reverse her car into a parking space. She had her back lights flashing and was doing a good job of it when a black BMW with two men up front poked its nose into her space. One of the men—obviously, shall we say, not British-born—got out and stood in the spot, while the driver just sat there. The lady got out and asked him what he was doing, saying, "I have two small children, for God's sake." He disdainfully waved her away and, arms crossed, stayed where he was. Although old enough to be the man's grandfather, I had to get involved. I walked over, telling the interloper sharply that I had seen the whole thing, that they had come long after she had begun to back into the parking space, and that he had no right to the space just because she was a woman. "Pull that crap where you come from," I concluded menacingly, "but not here." That did it. Like the bully-boy anarchists who intimidate the nation's politicians, the man started screaming and threatening. The poor woman whose spot they were trying to steal thanked me and wanted to leave, but I assured her that she should hold her ground, letting her know the man was all talk and no action. Sure enough, after more rants and threats, he and his buddy left. The lady was happy, and only one of the tots in the back cried.

It was a modest episode, to be sure, but all too representative of the times. Cowardice and solipsism are more highly valued today than decency and self-sacrifice, let alone courage or honor. And in large ways and small, women are the greatest victims of this loss.

When Axel von dem Bussche died on January 26, 1993, the obituaries were moving, but none of them caught the essence of the man, his warmth, the breadth of his interests, and the powerful effect he had on people. The subtext, unspoken, was that men like him are no longer the leaders of our society. Such a man understood that honor is all; in its absence civilization erodes and collapses.

We are now suffering the consequences of being led by a very different sort of people, those who have not served their country and do not honor its institutions, people who would never so much as renounce their creature comforts for the general good. Our dishonorable politicians lie and spin and think of only the next election; they who find their most fervent financial backers among the dishonorable purveyors of the vulgarity, sex, and violence that TV sends into our homes with devastating consequence for our children—the sort of filth that, if imposed by an unfriendly foreign power, might well be viewed as an act of war.

I'm no virgin, or easily shocked. I've covered wars, gambled with lowlifes, and hung out with tough hombres. But I cannot but wonder: How did we get to this point? Why are we allowing those who are supposed to lead and entertain us to bring us down to a level that would surprise even the hoodlums of old? Edmund Burke instructed that manners are more important than laws. I wonder how many of today's purported leaders or Hollywood biggies have ever so much as heard of him.

In an ideal world, men like Axel von dem Bussche would be our leaders.

Even try to imagine a world today that required those who declared a war to fight it. Churchill would have done it. Today? Viktor Orban, and any Polish leader, but that's about it.

Thankfully, the Greeks haven't yet reached the point where patriotism is regarded as something between a joke and an embarrassment among the young. Even now in Greek homes, the old stories are told and the words still spoken with reverence. Molon labe.

THIRTEEN

A Poor Little Greek Jailbird

In my long life, nothing was more instructive than the three months I spent as the Queen's guest in Pentonville prison. What did I learn?

That it is soul-destroying to cast oneself as a victim? No, I already knew that.

But something just as important, indeed a quality of manhood often far harder to come by, especially for those of us for whom much has always come easily.

Perseverance.

Life in prison teaches that you are, finally, on your own, so you'd better be self sufficient if you're going to survive in the face of life's upheavals.

I don't know if I'm physically brave, but after Pentonville I knew that I'd be able to take whatever life threw at me, pain, disappointment, betrayal, or loss.

Of course, the wife tells me that I'm quite lucky in choosing to remember just pleasant things, and it's true. For me memories are like beautifully edited copy, all cleaned up and retaining only the good parts. It is almost automatic—and the bad things are tucked away immediately, never to return. I suppose many idiots enjoy such forgetfulness, but then I'd rather be called an idiot than a surly grouch, which is what too many who face hard time become, destined to spend the rest of their days complaining and finding fault with everything and everyone.

It was on July 23, 1984, on reentering Britain, that I was busted at Heathrow for carrying stuffed in my back pocket two grams of cocaine I'd bought before my late-night flight from the barman at a downtown New York discotheque.

Passing through customs I was asked if I had anything to declare. "Nothing," I said, and was waved through.

Then, behind me, a voice said, "You're going to lose that envelope."

"Thank you," I replied. Then, being Taki, I added, "if only you knew what was in it."

He crooked a finger. "Come back here." And that was it.

I'd first tried cocaine in the late seventies, when the son of one of the richest Greek shipowners offered and insisted I take it. Before that, I'd never been involved at all with drugs. Growing up in the Fifties and even the Sixties no one was, at least not among the jocks and swells I knew.

The ones who took them were actors, artists, and other exotic types. Even in Vietnam I never touched the stuff. I was an athlete and a boozer, and as far as I was concerned drugs were for losers.

Until cocaine. I obviously liked it, and hanging around the nightclubs of the Eighties didn't exactly discourage me. Soon I began to buy it myself.

I had about eight hours to while away in a tiny six-by-four cell, as the reality of what I'd done descended on me, before I was to be brought before a magistrate in the morning. I tried to invent new karate techniques, but ended up just feeling sorry for myself.

When I appeared before the magistrate, my trial was set for two weeks hence.

I then drove to the country to contemplate what a fool I had made of myself. The bureau chiefs of AP and UPI tried to quash the story to prevent my father from finding out (who said all hacks were bad?), but it ran anyway, and the Greek press had a field day. "Fascist Son of Shipping Tycoon Busted" was probably the nicest.

I spoke to the editor of *The Spectator*, offering my resignation and apologizing for the embarrassment I'd caused the magazine, but he refused to take it and said just never do it again. As he told someone else, "If Taki were our religion correspondent I would have fired him on the spot. But as he is our High Life correspondent, we expect him to be high at times."

Of course, others were not of the same opinion, noting that as a conservative who'd been anti-drug in print, I'd made the rest of them look hypocritical. Point well taken.

At my trial, the prosecution did not demand a custodial sentence, since I had come clean right away and the drug was just for my personal use. The judge gave me four months anyway "so others of your class and background will begin to respect the laws of this country."

The judge was right. One cannot have two sets of laws, one for the rich and well-connected, another for the poor and dispossessed. The great Maggie Thatcher told me years later that she was appalled to hear that I might be deported upon my release, but she did nothing about it.

For her, too, rules were rules. For that was then.

Fortunately, my expulsion did not come to pass because of my previous exemplary conduct—not even the proverbial parking ticket on either side of the Atlantic.

In any case, I got four months, and soon after, with the ritual divesting of one's clothing and the issuing of two pairs of blue jeans and two blue-striped cotton shirts, followed by the first of many cold showers, I began my stay at Pentonville.

There was nothing left to do but serve my time.

And that's the test. Even for a short-termer who's been brought down several pegs, and maybe especially for one who is used to a more elegant lifestyle, it is imperative to be strong and positive, almost to try to kid yourself that there's something to be enjoyed about being inside. The happiest of the long-timers will tell you: Wake up each morning with a bit of zest and find something, however small, to look forward to that day.

There are those who consider Pentonville the worst prison in England, and I can see their point. The place is as grim as any medieval fortress, and it is as terrible an assault on the senses as a literal cesspool. Despite the popular conception that one can and will get used to anything, the stench of excreta remained as unbearable throughout my stay as it was at first whiff.

My cell, number D-31, was thirteen feet long, nine feet wide, and seven feet high—barely enough space for two steel beds and two chamber pots, since I was to share it with a roommate. (In Manhattan, people pay thousands for apartments this size, but that's another story.)

Still, I didn't find conditions all that bad. The food, for example.

White bread and porridge for breakfast, potatoes and dry ham for dinner, always accompanied by tea. That's the staple diet, and on special days pizza. (The smartest thing one can do is go vegetarian.)

While prison life is unremittingly bleak, I recall how physically well I felt during my time inside. The time in the slammer did wonders for my liver. Without boozing or drugs of any kind, lots of exercise and even more reading than usual, I was never healthier than during those three months in Pentonville. What else could a man wish for?

The contrast with Japan, where prisons are harsher and more primitive, which is to say punitive, is highly instructive. In the West, the do-gooders have turned prisons like Pentonville into low-life country clubs, with okay food, lots of exercise, and classes in just about anything. Ergo men are willing to do the time for their crime. There is none of that in Japan, and very little recidivism as a result.

Okay, there were no women. Yet when I think back I don't remember missing even them. Incredible as it may sound, that temporary absence was not entirely unwelcome. For while the pursuit of happiness is an unalienable right, as the Declaration of Independence has it, it is also true that in daily life more often than not those who try to deny us the pursuit of happiness are wives or girlfriends; replacements for the stern nannies, or even sterner mothers of our youth, the worst of whom we used to call ball-busters. By the time I entered Pentonville, I'd had women trying to thwart my pursuit of happiness throughout my life, mostly using the excuse that they were worried about my health. Why give a man hell after an occasional nightlong bender? Can't a man have a little fun once in a while?

The schedule was as follows: 6:30 a.m.—first bell; 7 a.m.—slop out, shave, and dress; 7:30 a.m.—breakfast; 8 a.m.—workshop; 11–11:45 a.m.—staggered shifts of exercise in the yard, then back to work; 1 p.m.—dinner; 1–2 p.m.—lockup; 2 p.m.—workshops; 4 p.m. tea, and then lockup for the night.

One of the grimmest parts was trying to keep clean. Prison is hot and sweaty, and the one bath a week is often in someone else's water. Your hair gets foul and falls out.

For all that, I recall some truly fun times among my fellow convicts. There was Warren, the large black man whose appeal I had to draw up because he was illiterate. Whining and lying to oneself is part of criminal behavior and like most every inmate, Warren blamed not himself but society or the fuzz. In his appeal he claimed that keeping him in jail denied the human rights of his four common-law wives who could not reach orgasm without him. "Are you dumb?" I said to him. "Don't you know that all English judges are prudes and they'll just increase your sentence?" Warren cried when he said goodbye to me. I left him a few cigarette packs and some socks.

In fact, looking back, much of the time I spent as Her Majesty's guest was good clean fun. Not all roses, of course. There are certain psychological barriers while one's doing bird that must be overcome, the most obvious ones being missing birthdays of loved ones, holidays, and so on. I am not among those who hate New Year's parties; in fact, on the contrary. So for me the worst New Year's ever was December 31, 1984. Talk about a party that never took off. Everyone was locked up by 7 p.m., and most of the jailbirds were asleep by the time the clock struck 12. I stayed up by force of habit, but all it did was make me more miserable.

At the same time, following that New Year's Eve I could feel the worst of my sentence was over. From then on it was only a matter of time and patience.

As I learned patience at the University of Pentonville, by studying the species I also learned much about strength and weakness, and loyalty and betrayal. In addition to being dirty, dumb, and dishonest, muggers, thugs, yobs, and criminals in general are terrific physical cowards. I'd go as far as to say that among my confederates there was not a single brave man to be found. They talked tough and swaggered a lot, but when push came to shove, they acted like the Saudi ruling gang. When they yelled or threatened, the thing to do was not yell back, but tell them in a quiet voice to go ahead and try it. Like the bum trying to steal the young mother's parking place, they almost never did.

Of course, you quickly learned not to trust anyone. If somebody offered you free tobacco, it was a good bet someone else would come up to you later and demand payment. (I wasted my money on cigarettes because I couldn't get the hang of rolling them.) I was early on advised that if I liked women, it was wise to stay far away from the three adjoining cells which constituted the "library" (though in fact one of the gay men who ran it proved helpful in finding me books that were not Westerns and had not been masturbated into).

Gym jobs were the best in the whole nick, and though they usually went to toughies, I was assigned to be gym orderly, handing out towels and sneakers to those who, not yet so resigned, wanted to try and stay in shape. But then I was transferred to a job sewing buttons on military uniforms. The supervisor soon complained about my woeful output, saying I was the worst he'd ever seen.

"Was Oscar Wilde any better?" I asked him, knowing the writer had spent time in Pentonville.

"You think I keep track of everyone who comes in here?" he replied irritably.

Probably not wise on my part, since like most people with no sense of humor, the warders were always on the lookout for being mocked, and some of them had it in for me to start with. A loss of mail privileges or time in isolation always loomed as a possibility. When they finally gave me my old job back, it made me happier than I'd been in years. Aside from allowing me to exercise, the gym contained Pentonville's only shower facilities.

Needless to say, my judge had it right—from the get-go, there was a naked unfairness to the whole system. My cellmate, Tony the Loon, was doing twelve years for a botched bank job after having ingested too much smack, and he still had six to go. (Low-life criminals get very nervous and, unlike their metropolitan elite counterparts who sniff coke, they take heroin.) Tony regarded me as an amateur and a fool for having got caught doing something that had no monetary reward and involved little danger. He openly smoked huge joints in our cell. Meanwhile, Lloyd, as in Blankfein, head of Goldman Sachs, will never do a single day and retire a billionaire.

Now I ask you: What kind of deal is that? Whatever happened to jailing white-collar crooks like the Goldman gang? Whatever happened to throwing out the bureaucrooks in Brussels who've encouraged such devastating financial shenanigans?

It is the same old story everywhere one looks. Crooks at the top—the bankers; crooks at the bottom—the central-casting types; and the middle classes whipsawed in the middle.

I'd always known it, of course, but there is a lot to be said for seeing it up close.

Decades after my term at Pentonville—for which I ended up serving three months of the four—I visited my friend Conrad Black whose criminal conviction, unlike my own, was entirely unjustified. Innocent of the charge of financial malfeasance, he was done in by a manifestly corrupt system, under political pressure. Never had it been more true that Judases betray and rats sell out. Yet when I visited him in Palm Beach as he was awaiting sentencing, he was the very picture of calm, good humor, and grace under pressure.

He would proceed to do his time and go on to more success and happiness.

Kipling said it for the ages:

> If you can fill the unforgiving minute
>   With sixty seconds' worth of distance run,
> Yours is the Earth and everything that's in it,
>   And—which is more—you'll be a Man, my son!

FOURTEEN

The Way to a Woman's Heart (and Bed)

THE SCENE was straight out of an F. Scott Fitzgerald story. I was dining with the writer Gay Talese at Elaine's, the legendary literary hangout, and had just gone outside into the chill evening for a cigarette, when two men and a lady with the looks of an upper-class flapper came out looking for a cab. They were well dressed and spoke proper English.

"I love you, I'll take you home," said one of the young men. "I love you more, let me take you home," said the other.

There was nothing else to do but to butt in, and I did. "I love you the most, and I've got a car and driver waiting."

No good this time. Although to their credit the two preppies laughed, from the lady I got a stare colder than the weather.

But I was pleased nonetheless. A moment had presented itself, and it had been properly seized, which is all one can ask for.

The three of them wandered off into the frigid night looking for a taxi. I went back in and had a very good evening with the writer and a beautiful model.

You see, in the endless, always enchanting interplay between men and the fairer sex, the goal is not so much the conquest as the quality of the effort.

Young men wonder endlessly how to win women. What are the tricks of seduction? Which strategies succeed and which result in egg on the face?

There is no formula for understanding, let alone winning a woman, and thank God for that. But this much is clear: It is masculinity to which femininity responds. Masculinity means making clear-cut decisions, being decisive, confidently good-humored, romantic, and self-directing.

Masculinity makes the womanizer. Not in the toned-body, preening-in-the-mirror, I-eat-shitake-mushrooms way, but in the self-reliant, non-whining, living-with-the-consequences-of-your-actions way. The Gables, Bogarts, Mitchums . . .

Nonetheless, there are in fact approaches that are more likely to bring success.

But let's start with a caveat. Nothing to follow should be confused with the amateurish, vulgar, and embarrassing "advice" put forth in the sub-literary genre of how-to guides on picking up women; for example, the inventory of the American Julien Blanc, self-anointed "international leader in dating advice." While in typical American style it has earned him a fortune, his guidance is meant for tattooed beer drinkers trying to pull drunken slags in cheap bars. Mine is for gentlemen endeavoring to make an impression on ladies and well-brought-up young women.

Although old fashioned seducers may no longer be le goût du jour—lady killers having been replaced as aspirational figures in the public mind by the very rich, who often look like Michael Bloomberg or even worse—they remain the great teachers. For human nature is immutable, so the paths into the hearts of the fairer sex are likewise eternal.

Obviously, there are qualities, starting with charm and humor but also including a genuine interest in others, that are innate. One either possesses them or, alas, not. Yet even these can to a certain degree be acquired by the attentive student. When I was a young man, Elsa Maxwell, the legendary gossip columnist, radio personality, and party giver extraordinaire, told me not to look as eager as I customarily did when meeting some sweet young thing. Well, what did Elsa know—she was born in 1881, while Wagner was scoring *Parsifal*. And, anyway, of course I looked eager, what else would I be? But it was good advice, and being headstrong and not following it cost me dearly. Even the young Taki had much to learn.

Many men of course give up the game before they even start, shying away from likely prey based on their own sense of inadequacy—unprepossessing looks or something else. This is a tragic misreading of the feminine sensibility, the happy fact being that women are far less superficial than we are, as well as much nicer—at least the better ones. And by nature they are disinclined to want to make a man feel bad—though this is less true in the age of feminism than it once was.

Indeed, on the evidence, many of them scarcely care about looks at all. While if Helen of Troy had been ugly we Greeks would not have gone to war for ten days to get her back, let alone ten years, Willy Rizzo, a photographer I hung out with in Paris during the Fifties, was very short, squinted nonstop, and looked like a defrocked priest, yet he had to fight them off. Amazing as it is, most women really do prefer brains and charm. The eighteen-century British politician John Wilkes, himself no Brad Pitt, summed it up by saying that thirty minutes alone with any lady was enough to overcome his ugliness and leave him triumphant over any far better-looking rival.

That said, of course one never wants to find oneself competing with the likes of Brad—or, even more so, Errol Flynn, as great a seducer as there ever was. Although friendly with his son, I only met the elder Flynn once, in El Morocco, and he was very drunk. Still, the girl I was with went weak at the knees, and I had to be quick on my feet to maneuver her away from him.

But what's key is that he had great charm to go along with his great looks, and was very well read. Both his parents were academics, and he could reel off a poem that would make any girl's head spin. Bottom line: He'd have done nearly as well with Willy Rizzo's looks.

Casanova himself was no looker. He was bald and had a pot belly. But he was the ultimate possessor of what might be called craveability, the knack of convincing a woman that she cannot live without him, and he without her. Old Giacomo had that talent in spades.

How so?

Quite simply, he understood that women's emotional reactions are profoundly different from those of men. To put it in contemporary terms, they like romance, men like porn. Read his memoirs—he understood this essential truth to the very depths of his being. And his every word and gesture followed from that understanding.

This, indeed, is what is behind all the supposed tricks of the seducer's trade: the simple understanding that there is a way to treat women, and some men have it and others don't.

So, under the general heading of Know Your Prey . . .

- The fairer sex respect strength and despise weakness. Anything that smacks of pleading is an absolute no-no. Never harass, never beg, never overly insist. Women, real women, adore the strength of womanizers.

- Women are curious and easily intrigued, and what better way to intrigue them than to leave them alone to think of you? While, as Elsa Maxwell so sagely advised, being too eager can put off a lady, she is likely to be enticed by strategic disappearance. For one who has come on strong romantically, an unexpected, very polite good-night accompanied by the expression of a wish to see her again is very potent.
- Another sine qua non is don't talk about yourself, ask her about herself instead. Her job, her dreams, her likes or dislikes.
- But never, but never, ask about her boyfriend, husband, or lover. Pretend that she's never had any of the three. Never give her time to think of him because, again unlike us, women have a conscience.
- And—need it be said?—never talk about another woman.
- If the one you want is resisting you, flirt with the girl-friend. Not too much, just enough to allow the object of your affection to go further.
- Women love flattery, and successful seducers are assiduous flatterers. The man who writes heartfelt love letters to a woman is not only romantic and lyrical, he is also smart.
- As Casanova himself advised, always flatter the beautiful for their intelligence, and the intelligent for their beauty.
- Never admit anything, for all their protestations real women don't want to know. And women who don't know don't spill beans.
- Quote Lorenzo Da Ponte, not Karl Marx.

In the end, the key to everything is having a genuinely romantic nature. And in this regard, the times we live in, where boorishness and vulgarity are the rule, work to the seducer's advantage.

For in an age where the drunken gropings of seedy would-be lotharios too often put the stronger sex to shame, the gentleman's contrast with others could hardly be more striking. Rare as they are these days, good manners reflect an inner unselfishness, and the readiness to put others first. To a woman, they are the opposite of brute force, and highly romantic.

Among the most genuinely polite men I've ever known, especially to ladies, was my friend Vladimir, whose charm lay in his sincerity. No one was more successful a seducer, while looking more innocent. He would leave Gstaad after having seduced a maid, stop in Montreux and sleep with, say, a seamstress, go on to Lausanne where he would have a roll in the hay with a schoolteacher, then have a quickie in Geneva with a diplomat's wife, and come back to Gstaad that evening. The only bad thing about him was his constant efforts to steal my girls, but even that was done with great style and finesse.

This brings me to the ultimate weapon for seducing a woman: the grand romantic gesture. Desire in a woman has many faces. She can be moved by a smile, an image, a phrase. But nothing moves her more than a profession of love—even if unspoken. Saying it out loud does not work, at least not for the kind of woman that interests me. But there are other ways. Granted, in the current cynical age, some will be dismissed as corny. But, once again, that will be to the seducer's advantage. My old mentor, Porfirio Rubirosa, used to sing while strumming a guitar in an outdoor nightclub in the south of France, and it was irresistible to women then, and would be today. For his effortless charm will never be dated.

Too, with the right woman the right music is always a collaborative adventure. It brings shared emotional reactions to the fore, lust or joy or sorrow, for music is pegged to one's heart. That's why the modern cacophony that too often passes for music nowadays is so soulless.

This is not to suggest that all modern music is worthless. After a late night a few years back, I went to a Broadway matinée on my own. It was *Jersey Boys*, the story of Frankie Valli and the Four Seasons, a hit show with tunes that slam one with waves of nostalgia and longing. One particular song, "My Eyes Adored You," almost knocked me out.

Perhaps it was the hangover, but most likely it was Pam Wallin, a beautiful Palm Beach girl who once walked barefoot onto the plane on which I was leaving the beach for New York, just to say goodbye. In those more innocent days a pretty girl could walk on and off a plane undisturbed, and this one had a fetching boy's haircut and the best legs in Florida. An older boy at Lawrenceville was her beau, but he was at Lehman Brothers while I was in Palm Beach. He hated me at school and his hatred grew after graduation. But "My Eyes Adored You" was our song, Pam's and mine, and all these years later I listened to it and thought of Pam and Taki dancing at Taboo and at the Alibi. I almost cried.

Speaking of atmospherics—nowhere, not even Paris, beats Athens at its best. A very long time ago, still in my teens, I knew a beautiful Athenian girl whose eyes were green and hair golden blonde, and she too was in love with a friend of mine. But then he went away to school in Switzerland, and you can guess the rest. I stood by her, listening to her laments late at night, and then, one evening under a moonlit Acropolis, we kissed. She told me she felt guilty for having done it, but on we went, the moon, the ruins, the gentle breezes all helping me along. It was a case of patience and perfect timing. (The retsina also helped.)

If you visit Athens, you will see. Like the girl on the Acropolis, she will welcome you with open arms and then some.

Still, over the years nothing has worked so well for me as the written word. I've written earlier of the success I had quoting Shakespeare in my famous R&J letter. Repetition, of course, diluted its power, and after my original success, I probably overdid it. There are hundreds of letters declaring "Heaven is here, where Juliet lives," getting yellower by the minute, and someone even suggested that the original could be worth a lot. But never mind. The R&J letter invariably served as excellent artillery to soften up the target, and when it was nice and soft, the cavalry charged with: "Heaven without you would be too much to bear, and hell would not be hell if you were there."

If she could resist that one, it was time to give up and stop wasting both our time.

Naturally, I'm asked often about pickup lines. The general rule here is simple: What matters is less the line than the quality of the delivery, which is to say the attitude of the deliverer. Under the wrong circumstances the best line will seem trite, or, worse, reek of desperation, whereas even idiotic words delivered with a wry smile and twinkling eye will register a direct hit. For humor—and, above all, self-deprecation—reflect that most manly of manly traits, confidence.

I recently had dinner with the prettiest girl in London, and I introduced her around as the future Mrs. Taki. The fact that I've been happily married for more than fifty years is beside the point, and a very bourgeois point, to boot. If she gives me the go-ahead, things can change overnight.

In short, make a girl laugh and you're halfway there.

A joke, even a lame joke, can serve a useful purpose, especially on first meeting. What matters is the follow-up, where you might admit you've been rehearsing it since you first spotted her at the start of the evening. It's sort of a test. If she's any good she'll love it.

Of course, the best pickup line is one that doesn't feel like a pickup line. My friend James Toback tells me that when trolling in Hollywood, where the target is likely to be a pretty young aspirant, his go-to line is a sincere "What are you missing in your life?" quickly followed by, "What can I do to make your life better?" "Anyone not responding to that is not worth picking up," he declares.

My German cook Daniel, who besides being a very good cook was as good a pickup artist as I ever came across in my travels, understood innately the importance of locale in the success of a line. His specialties were English and Dutch girls in the south of France, and his best line was a sad, sincere: "I know you will not like me because I'm German, but you will come on board for a drink . . . ja?"

One summer in Porto Heli, off the Peloponnese, with Alexandra in Gstaad and the children gallivanting somewhere in Europe, Daniel put his magic to work. He picked up four female sailors, two of them quite beautiful, and brought them on board my boat. The evening was a great success until neighboring boats heading off for a morning sail began to hoot their horns as they watched me and my crew dead drunk on deck trying to fondle fellow sailors.

Daniel broke my heart when he decided he wanted to leave me to travel and see the world. "What's there to see?" I told him. "There's nothing but vulgar oligarchs and semi-criminal sports stars out there."

It was in Saint-Tropez that I once discovered what seemed the pickup line to end all pickup lines. "Hello, again," I would shout at everyone I saw, and the line worked as if by magic. Partly it was that everyone was more or less always stoned in Saint-Tropez, so the word "again" meant that we had already been properly introduced, and perhaps even been intimate. There were smiles of recognition, however faint. It probably also helped that I was accompanied on that visit by Sir Bob Geldof. Still, the line stood the test of time. Even Sir Bob himself was amazed. "He's effing eighty effing years old, and his effing line effing works," he announced.

Of course, one can go too far. One very early morning in Britain, after a hell of an evening, I was being driven to Badminton, and at a gas station on the M4 I encountered a beautiful young woman. My attempted pickup line, it seems, for I was later told, was to ask if she wanted to meet King Constantine of the Hellenes, who I claimed was traveling with me. (It surprised even me that I would use the king of my country as bait.) According to my actual traveling companions, she declined, bid me adieu, and went on her way. But, she at least told them that I was very polite.

The most amusing pickup artist I've ever been privileged to watch in action was my friend Yanni Zographos. He had a "system" for picking up women with young children in tow. As he passed a mother pushing a pram he would loudly announce to no one in particular, "Les jolies mamans font des jolies bébés . . ." Heads would turn and the woman in question would naturally smile. Starting in the summer of 1956, my first free year after eleven years in academic captivity, I put his theory to the test, and I can confirm that in the nearly sixty ensuing years neither Yanni nor I ever managed to pick up a single woman with that line. Still, we always remained upbeat and confident.

Another favorite would-be pickup line of Yanni's back in the Fifties was to yell "taxi!" while riding up and down Athens in his Bentley convertible, offering taxi rides to women. The theory was that, since Greece had only about two thousand cars in total back then, and public transport was crowded and unreliable, our targets would find such an offer irresistible. Yet again, I can confirm that in the forty years leading up to his death neither he nor I ever managed to persuade a single member of the female sex to get into the bloody Bentley.

But, again—for this cannot be overly stressed—what mattered was the attitude, the sheer devil-may-caredness of it all. For his lousy pickup tactics notwithstanding, in the general scheme of things Yanni did very well, his raw confidence invariably having the desired effect on the fairer sex.

Others in my circle had equally offbeat approaches that sometimes actually worked. My friend Nicola used to pretend that he was a virgin and had to go with a woman before doing his military service. More than one girl fell for it. Mine, unfortunately, did not, or at least so she told me.

I confess that I myself have never been a master of pickup arts; what successes I've enjoyed have usually involved the times I've won some sweet young thing's favor basically playing it for laughs. Yet tellingly this has proven easier as I've grown older. Ever since I began to look my age, I've become even more polite than usual, and when the opportunity arises, I approach the lady or ladies in question to ask, with a smile, if any of them might be interested in a much older man. In all the years I've been trying this, all but one has said yes—though, alas, usually laughingly. Less is expected of the older gentleman, and while promises are easily made, they are also more easily broken.

One late evening in the bar of Washington's Willard Hotel, where presidents Grant and Harding used to get up to no good, a friend and I ran into a congressman from Indiana sitting with three sweet young things. The mother of my children was asleep upstairs, which inspired my friend to tell the youngest of the ladies that I was married to an eighty-seven-year-old whose father had put a curse on me which said that I would have to stay hitched to his eighty-seven-year-old daughter until a very young woman decided to marry me. Pathetic tale that it was, it worked. Well, sort of. The twenty-two-year-old assistant to the Indiana congressman felt very sorry for me, and agreed that she would help me lift the curse from my wicked father-in-law. Not now, but at some point. So I say there's still hope—even as the friend who started it continues to dine out on the story.

On a recent visit to London, two lovely girls happened to drop by the place where I was staying. One of them was a tall English girl I had met once before but much too briefly, the other an American from Los Angeles. My hostess had kindly put me between them and, even if I say so myself, I didn't do too badly. My plan was a simple one. By playing the clown I thought I had a chance with Los Angeles, my friend Jeffrey Bernard having once told me a blonde secretary from that hellhole had taken him to her bed when he passed out on her shoulder.

Unfortunately, what worked for Jeff did not for Taki. When I made my move she (LA) declared that if I wasn't such a clown I might have had a chance with her, but not tonight thank you. In a panic I turned to the English girl but she also let me down. Something to do with being asked second, I imagine.

This is not to suggest that the aging lothario of zesty spirit does not enjoy at least some advantages. I was great friends with the actor Roger Moore, one of the better James Bonds, when I was confronted with a situation involving his youngest son. He was seventeen, as devastatingly handsome as his father, and circling a blonde I was quite chummy with. "Christian Moore keeps calling me," she said. "He's very good-looking."

I looked at her with the grave concern of the elder statesman. "I hope he's good-looking enough to go to jail for," I said. "He's just thirteen, you know."

Other things may fade, and we may have to cheat a bit, but as long as we've got our wits, we oldies know how to protect our turf.

FIFTEEN

This Connoisseur's Ideal Woman

THERE'S A game I used to play nonstop with my great friend Gianni Agnelli, the long gone head of Fiat. I'd throw out a name of a woman we both knew (knew, that is, well enough to dislike), and Gianni would comment on the man she would hypothetically end up with: "A pimp" or "semi-gentleman" usually. But the worst was: "Poor, poor man, he'll never know what hit him."

It wasn't nice but it was fun, and in any case the assessments were grounded in experience. We each had a keen sense of who was to be avoided at all costs.

Otherwise, where the fair sex was concerned, we parted ways. Gianni liked women as much as I do, but we each had our types. His were big, brassy, and sexy, like Anita Ekberg, the Swedish bombshell who was his mistress for ages. Mine were sweet, young, and innocent. Gianni looked for the film-noir type,

I was more of a dreamer. I once brought the beautiful wife of an Englishman onto his boat—we had run off together for a dirty weekend—and overheard him describe her to a fellow guest: "She's rather sweet, like those football wives I have to give dinner to at times," he said rather dismissively. (At the time Gianni owned the top-tier Juventus club.) In fact, the lady in question was upper class and restrained in her opinions, which in Gianni's world-weary eyes made her a footballer-moll.

The long and the short of it is, I don't like slags. For me, there is nothing more beautiful to behold than an innocent and feminine woman, someone who hasn't been around the block too many times. Such women are not to be found in Hollywood or Monte Carlo or Mykonos.

They don't make a big house their priority, or big yachts, which are a better measure of one's wealth. They are found in proper homes with proper parents and a dog or two (and ponies). Show me a sweet young thing who turns red when complimented and who prefers a sailing boat to a gin palace and I will leave the wife tomorrow.

An English newspaper once asked me to write a few hundred words on my perfect woman to end up with on a desert island—someone who would not only stave off the monotony of ivory beaches and coconuts but provide monogamous sex at will. I wrote that to be continually interesting to me, a woman must be reserved and self-possessed on the outside, while smoldering underneath.

My friend Irwin Shaw wrote a wonderful short story, the title of which, "Girls in Summer Dresses," sums up my feelings exactly. For summer is etched in my psyche as the time for such girls. Long ago memories of "girls in their summer dresses" provoke in me a surge of pure longing. One's senses are more acute in summer—the acrid tang of heat emanating from the sidewalks of New York or Paris, the breezes of late afternoon, the whiff of perfume of a passing beauty. One falls in love quicker in summertime. In one's youth summertime was a dress rehearsal of coming manhood, the realization that sooner or later one would fall desperately in love and lie drugged with pleasure on the grass with the girl of one's dreams.

And all these many years later, that feeling has never left me.

This is not to say that my ideal must not also have certain qualities deemed masculine, like strength of character, rationality, and firmness.

Good feminine women can be feisty, indomitable, and tomboys, all adding to and not detracting from, their allure. But those qualities should not dominate. Because above all she must remain feminine. A woman lacking femininity cannot possibly be considered beautiful in the true and classical sense of the word.

It should not have to be said—though given the times, probably must be—that spouting swear words and bombast is not feminine, and that a grating voice ruins an otherwise beautiful face. One of the true horrors of modern life is hearing an attractive young woman effing this and effing that and saying "like" before every word. Some American women's very voices are to femininity what gangsta rap is to Mozart, high-pitched shrieks, like a hyena being strangled. (Though while I have been aurally assaulted by such noise time and again in America, I've never heard such a sound in Africa.)

I miss the way American girls used to be: bright, clever, sweet, full of energy, resourceful, blonde, beautiful, and with perfect teeth, even at a time when few people flossed. But that was long ago. Now we have screeching, high-pitched voices, hard looks, and ugliness à la Harvey Weinstein.

Not long ago, lost in Byronic thoughts while visiting the Acropolis, I noticed three young women speaking with American accents and taking selfies as they posed in a stripper's come-on manner. I approached them and introduced myself as a morality policeman safeguarding sacred grounds from foreign sacrilege. I've never seen three more terrorized beings. "This is simply a warning," I said severely. "The Acropolis is not a strip joint."

How, then, to find the sought-for paragons of perfection?

George Jean Nathan was a great American critic, but he was no romantic. He said that what a man ought to look for in a woman is something like a good piano, minus the loud pedal: sturdy, reliable, and able to make beautiful music when called upon. But of course it is also true that there are some women who are all pedal, without tone or modulation; and others whose appearance might be unprepossessing, but in whom the sensitive ear will discern gentler strains beneath.

The perfect woman in my eyes? In truth, it depends when you ask, for the ideal model of my heart's desire changes with some regularity. In the general category of actresses, for instance, my obsessions have ranged from Ava, as in Gardner, to Zellweger, Renée, and including at various times Juliette Binoche, Helen Hunt, and Ashley Judd. For a time I daily lusted after Rebecca Hall, hoping to trap her in some igloo and keep her there for the duration. (As much as anything it was the slight physical imperfections in Rebecca that drove me mad with desire.) The mother of my children called me sick, but I was as healthy as a young horse, and almost as randy.

Later it was Keira Knightley, and then, temporarily foregoing actresses, *The Spectator*'s own winsome deputy editor, to whom I publicly announced the happy news of our engagement, only to learn that she had betrayed me by betrothing herself to someone else. It was the worst defeat since Stalingrad.

But in short order I rebounded with a new-found love: Jessica Raine, who played the graceful and shy nurse Jenny in the Sunday-night soap *Call the Midwife*. This was the kind of coup de foudre I hadn't experienced in years. Cupid's arrow pierced my breast one Sunday evening, and I didn't have a peaceful night's sleep for months afterward. I had my daughter Google Jessica, and received the intelligence she grew up on a Welsh farm near Powys. "She's very pretty and nice," even the mother of my children admitted, however reluctantly.

What first attracted me was the role she played. Her grace, shyness, and understatement, her intense and repressed character, were straight out of some Terence Rattigan play. And I loved her rather plain beauty—an English rose, not one of those grotesque tarts who fall out of their bras while drunk and stumble in their ghastly Louboutins, the ugliest shoes ever invented by men who hate women.

Nurse Jenny's total lack of flamboyance and inability to be vulgar even if she tried had me loathing myself for having fallen for others in the past. I swore that from now on and until the day I died it would be only Jessica Raine and Nurse Jenny, to whom my heart and soul belong. She could have anything of mine, boat included, if she'd agree to have a dinner—one single dinner in Paris—with no après dinner tricks, unless of course . . . but I didn't dare dream that far ahead. I even offered a very nice present to anyone who'd show her the article making the offer, and an even nicer one to anyone who'd arrange the dinner.

The King of Greece, among others, made fun of me about my Jessica obsession. "While Your Majesty laughs, I suffer," was all I said to him. But I produced a couple of pictures of her cut out from the *Daily Telegraph* and left them beside his dinner plate, which to my mind made the point.

In brief, for me Jenny was the incarnation of goodness, and her enchanting looks turned me into a foolish erotomaniac. Sanctity is a woman's ideal and it is based on passion, which by means of love lifts us above law. Jessica-Jenny played this kind of character. I liked to think that no one could be so great an actress as to be angelic as she appeared on screen and be a slut in real life.

Well, in an unspeakable act of cruelty, the deputy editor not only went ahead and got married, she also hunted down Jessica Raine and commissioned a piece from her for *The Spectator*, wherein she admitted to being perturbed by what I wrote about her. She advised me to cool my jets, and otherwise plunged in the knife. This to a man who had not only kept a laminated picture of Nurse Jenny on her bike close at hand, but also left copies of it on tables of strangers, the way handicapped people do.

All right, then, I grimly decided, let Jessica-Jenny go with men her age and listen to monologues about football or other such rubbish! Let them lurch drunkenly toward her, unlike an older gent like me who would give up drink on the day, now that's never going to happen. And let's see who among my rivals will weave thousands of blossoms and use weathered green trellis lit from behind to simulate dining under a huge wisteria tree, the plan I had for Paris.

Worse still, I could almost trace a lawyer's thoughts when she wrote about "being compelled to bring him back to reality."

Enough said. The point, as a terribly nice Swiss village doctor once said to me, is there's nothing to be done. His diagnosis: "There is nothing you can take to relieve that pleasant ache; you're not sick, you're just in love."

Quite simply the frontals of my brain trigger me off when I see enchanting females like Jessica. The only treatment might be the one tried on that Kennedy girl whose father, the kind Joseph Kennedy, used when he had her lobotomized.

My wife thinks I should be lobotomized, but my children think it's too much. One thing is for sure. I will not leave it up to the love of my life that could have been, even if the kind nurse Jenny would look after me after the operation.

Needless to say, we're all slaves to our genes, and for a man being oversexed is a necessary condition of the well-lived life. Yet by itself it is not nearly enough. One must also have a degree of emotional illiteracy.

This is why there are exceptions to even the truest of truisms. Yes, beauty is synonymous with youth, and the yearning to recapture the feelings one experienced recalling one's own—for instance, the scent of a once young and beautiful Virginia girl named Mary Blair—are ever present.

Yet it is also true that in the pursuit of the fairer sex one must remain open to possibilities that may arise at any time, or any place.

Not long ago, I was seated at lunch between a beautiful mother and her seventeen-year-old daughter. To my surprise, as well as that of the mother of my children who was watching me like a hawk, I preferred the mother. It was her voice that seduced me. The lady in question lives in Ireland, has three daughters and a very nice husband to whom she's happily married. My task would seem a hard one. But really I only want to hear her voice. By the end of lunch she had agreed to accept my telephone calls and read out the Irish telephone book if need be.

But that's an exception to the general rule. In the normal course of things, youth almost always does win the day.

At another lunch soon after, I was seated next to an even more beautiful version of Ashley Judd named Diane G., and it was love at first sight. She had a body slightly reminiscent of a Matisse drawing, but sculpted: the patrician feet, beautiful legs and arms, hooded blue eyes, an upper-class insouciance, perhaps a bit contrived—in other words, the perfect mistress.

I attacked immediately.

"I have six months to live. It's nothing contagious, or disgusting, but I only have six months left. Will you marry me? You can have it all after that."

Diane: "What about your kids?"

Me: "They're already taken care of."

Diane: "And the mother of your children?"

Me: "She's taken care of."

Diane: "What about if you live longer?"

Me: "You keep it all and I will disappear."

Diane: "In that case we might have a deal."

Happiness is the moment when the faint whisper of hope is about to become reality. I was in a hell of a state. What a beauty! Nothing could quench the thirst of my lust—and then disaster.

John-Taki, my own flesh and blood, came and plonked himself next to her.

"Who is this?" she asked.

"My son. He's twenty-two and a painter in Paris."

"I think we no longer have a deal," she whispered.

SIXTEEN

The Languages of Love

AND NOW we come to the matter of place. Should an aspiring lothario take country (and culture) into account in determining the object and nature of his pursuit?

Was the Draft Dodger a shameless cad?

Professor Harold Hill in *The Music Man* said it best: "You gotta know the territory." For though certain truths obviously hold for women and men everywhere, there are vast differences in attitude regarding the hows, whys, and wherefores.

With that in mind, a quick rundown by nationality, based on observation and, more important, experience.

Americans: What to say? Under the tyranny of feminism, all that was once beautiful has turned crude. There are no more ladies and gentlemen in America, only men and women. But the "aristocracy of everyone" simply doesn't work. The basics of life cannot be codified and legislated, especially when it comes to matters romantic and sexual. And this the harridans will never accept, they are in a war to the death with biology, and they rule the roost.

In short, with a few exceptions, American women are to be avoided at all costs. They are like German Panzer commanders: aggressive and always on the offensive. I admire aggressive soldiers, but I don't want them in my bed.

Even those left largely untouched by the feminist scourge can be problematic, as they tend to be overly concerned with presentation—clothes, makeup, body tone—and too little with heart, brains, and grace.

Needless to say, this is especially so in the hellhole that is Southern California, where surfing, sunbathing, and exercising make more or less perfect bodies, but far from perfect women. Unlike those surf-riding beachboy dummies, I do not wish they could all be California girls.

Your best bet are Southern belles, but even among these, those untouched by present-day coarseness are increasingly hard to find.

On top of the rest, there is the traditional American morality, with its excessive stress on guilt and shame. Once caught with their pants down, American men usually make a public confession and act contrite because in America cheating on a girl means one is also capable of being corrupt in business and stealing from church collections for the poor.

I've heard of businessmen confessing to their employees for having cheated on their wives. No wonder business ain't what it used to be in the land of plenty!

French: The French make it very hard for one to defend them. They are arrogant and unfriendly. On the plus side, however, they are masters of seduction and excelled in the sexual liberation of women while the Americans were still burning so-called witches. So they die laughing about the American obsession with confession and much else.

Cynicism is a national trait, and they practice it with gusto.

Arletty, the great French star of the silver screen during the Thirties and Forties, put it as well as anyone. Accused of having had sex with a German officer during the Occupation, she replied frankly, "My heart is French, but my arse is international."

The principal trait in the character of a Frenchwoman is an exaggerated coquetry, carried to so great an extent that it can never be reconciled with true love. This is in contrast to German women. Cold at the start but ever practical, they are increasingly attracted and attached as they discover good qualities in their lover.

For their part, most French men feel that not to try is an insult to a woman. So, I believe, do the women. Moreover, men in France consider a mistress to be a normal part of a male's panoply, which is also all to the good. A romantic man will flirt with a woman he finds attractive.

Graciously, if grudgingly, he will accept it when she refuses him. It is always a lady's choice. No ifs or buts about it. And the well-bred man accepts her choice with a courtly flourish.

Take my case, for example. There was a certain young demoiselle on whom I cast my eye, and it was a case of doing as the locals do. I tried my best to flirt with her. I once rang her from Budapest and got her mother instead. So no good, and in the end I grudgingly accepted the fact that I was not old enough for her.

It was about twenty years or so ago that I took part in a debate about whether Britain would be better off siding with Paris or Washington where foreign policy was concerned. The egregious George W. Bush was in the White House and Washington's foreign policy was being run by neocons. When my turn came, I said that London should follow the land of le fromage for the simple reason that Paris had Catherine Deneuve, Juliette Binoche, and Irène Jacob, whereas America had Hillary Clinton, Shirley MacLaine, and Jane Fonda. I think that won it for my side.

At a French embassy drinks party afterward, the ambassador thanked me for bringing up France's women, as well he might. He couldn't very well bring up the country's fighting men in World War II, could he? Soon after, Catherine Deneuve once again came to the rescue, denouncing the #MeToo witch hunt as being no less phony than the one that burnt those poor women in Salem long ago. She and others signed an open letter published in *Le Monde* attacking the wave of neo "puritanism" then engulfing America and injecting some badly needed truths into Hollywood's bullshit.

My first mistress, as well as my first wife, were French. My present wife was born in Paris and grew up there. Fearful of a certain painful nostalgia, I try now to avoid the City of Light. Even so, when I am forced to be there, I am never saddened by encounters with old lovers, however much they've aged. French women cope with age in the same manner in which they handle errant husbands, unfaithful lovers, and conniving friends—with aplomb. And most important, one never feels guilty with French women. This is because they are as discreet as the men, and one never knows what they've done behind your back.

English: All the clichés are true. Lack of sunshine makes English people dour and desperately lacking in Dionysian abandon. Their state of existence seems to be one of catatonic recumbency in a darkened room.

In a word, the English have great difficulty understanding passion.

Anna Karenina is incomprehensible to them. To give up a loving husband, a child, and a beautiful stately pile for an officer strikes them as madness. They are simply too horsey, too suppressed, too class conscious.

Yet—and this is not a contradiction—English girls give it away like a Frisbee. What's an eighteen-year-old English virgin like?

Nobody knows. What's a thirteen-year-old English virgin like? Ask a Turkish waiter.

A recent study has found that Britain is numero uno in Europe in one-night stands. You think? Researchers claim the high one-night score reflects "society's greater tolerance of sexual promiscuity among women as well as men." "Rubbish," says Taki, the greatest sex researcher since Kinsey. It is linked to one and one thing only: alcohol. British gals booze, while Greek lassies, for instance, do not. Last time I saw a Greek girl drunk was some time in the Sixties. Last time I saw an English girl drunk was the last time I was in London.

English girls need a lot more exposure to their French counterparts.

Just as Paris should be a part of every red-blooded young man's education, so should it be for every young Sloane. It would transform them overnight.

Which brings me to the English and their trouble with sex—English men, that is. While the English tabloids may be full of stories about "drug-fueled sex sessions" and three-in-a-bed situations, sex is seen by the average English male not as good fun, but as something to be practiced in a dark room and only in the missionary position. And whereas when the typical Gallic pair indulge in a ménage à trois it is in the expected fashion (even the loathsome Sartre and Beauvoir included another woman, a younger lesbian), the Brits prefer their ménages with another man. British lefties and wets can only get it up with two men and a woman watching.

Taki's advice? Fuckers of England unite. You have nothing to lose but your inhibitions.

Italians: There is a reason so many Anglos have gone to live in the Land of Pasta and never returned to the Land of Fish and Chips. How many tourists have suffered from Stendhal syndrome when visiting Leeds? How many English restaurants do we know in Italy?

Italians accept life as it is. They don't accost you about smoking, they don't lecture you about the evils of red meat. Ideological fads like "multiculturalism" have largely passed them by. They are also the least credulous people in the world. They do not trust politicians and in return pols promise nothing because they know they will not be believed. In Italy, governments bribe contractors and contractors bribe governments, and nobody claims they're totally honest. Life is what it is and always has been. When it gets too hot everyone goes to the beach. The country itself is one long pleasure. Their greatest political thinker, Machiavelli, did not bother himself with individual rights. His was a skeptical philosophy, a guide to survival in a world filled, as it was and always will be, with liars, brigands, and cutthroats.

And so goes their attitudes sexual. Men and women know what the opposite sex is meant for, and don't overthink it.

So come south, sweetheart, and as Yogi Berra put it, each day "it's déjà vu all over again." Macho men rule supreme.

Greeks: Suddenly young Greek women are among the most attractive in Europe. I kid you not. Greek girls were always among the sexiest in the world—there is no such thing as a Greek female who is lousy in bed—but they were also quite ugly, short, fat, and terribly hairy. But Zeus must have pulled quite a trick, because they have been transformed overnight—and are now tall, chic, slim, with lovely legs, and still great in the sack.

My friend Leonidas Goulandris, son of Professor Johannes Goulandris of Heidelberg University, insists that Greek girls are as horny as they are because of the steady diet of sugarless baklava, pistachios, and retsina. I think it's the climate. Either way, what an irony it would be if the newly beautiful lost their special quality. That's what I would call a real Greek tragedy.

Spaniards: I was once promenading during the Feria in Seville, accompanied by an American woman who was attractive, but in the bland Bo Derek kind of way. And I was suddenly struck by the way the Spanish women in flamenco dresses walked. Latin women walk like women, hips gliding, heads held high. It is an inherent trait of rhythm and grace. Even plain women are seductive and lovely.

My designer friend Carolina Herrera comes to mind. She is the essence of femininity, but makes it look easy, like Joe DiMaggio striding after a fly ball. Yet it's all done with mirrors. She works harder than most men I know, even as the most important things in her life are her husband and children.

Polish: No one outdoes the Poles for grace and charm. Just before the war, Mussolini's foreign minister and son-in-law, Count Ciano and his wife Edda visited Warsaw, where a Polish colonel asked the couple if they would take supper with him in the regimental mess. After supper the colonel asked Countess Ciano whether she would care to dance.

When she said yes, the curtains were drawn aside to reveal a jazz band and eighteen Polish officers in full dress uniform. As the band began to play, the eighteen Polish officers bowed and simultaneously asked her to dance.

Edda then got up and danced with each and every one of them. She called it the most romantic and dashing evening ever.

Trust the Poles to have achieved it. A few random observations:

- Latin Americans are particularly good at handling infidelity, with **Dominicans** among the biggest cheaters.
- It was only in 1991 that **Brazil's** Supreme Court declared that a husband could no longer murder his adulterous wife and her lover. (Phew!) The widow I was dancing with à trois last week was married to a Brazilian, now resting in peace, but one never knows.

- In **Russia** both men and women cheat. Living in two-room apartments with a large family does not for peaceful sex make. Russians have sex in order to have a break from the bickering. Crooked oligarchs living in London do not have sex because their houses are too big and by the time they find their tarts the urge is gone.
- The **Germans** and the **Japanese** have turned from warriors into merchants, as disgusting a transformation as I can think of. The results in the bedroom are predictable.

And then, the worst of the worst.

There are no laws in **Saudi Arabia** defining the minimum age for marriage, as the conservative Muslim clergy oppose any attempt to end child marriages. I read not long ago that an eight-year-old Saudi girl divorced her middle-aged husband after her father forced her to marry the pig in exchange for $13,000. No wonder all these rogue male Saudis descend upon our shores and ogle our women, especially during Royal Ascot. Living with a child can be tiresome.

I also read that a Saudi court had sentenced a journalist to sixty lashes after she was charged with involvement in a TV show in which a Saudi man had talked about sex. My first thought was to imagine what it will be like if and when Sharia law comes to America or Britain, and watching all the ghastly leftist producers of reality programs being whipped nonstop for presiding over hate shows.

SEVENTEEN

Taking the Fatal Plunge (Part One)

One Valentine's Day, I ran into the King of Greece in the local bank asking a teller where he could buy a Valentine card for his queen. After forty-seven years of marriage, I was pleased to learn that even kings bought Valentine cards for their queens. I was quite touched.

I've been in trouble with women throughout my long life. That's because I like them so much I can't keep my hands off them. But this does not mean I'm not a proponent of marriage. To the contrary, there is no social institution I regard as more vital. Marriage attaches a child's parents to each other and in turn attaches the couple to the child.

Unmarried couples do not stick around when the going gets tough. Once either parent takes off, the child invariably gets into drugs, booze, and delinquency. Fatherless children means fragmented families, delinquent behavior, and the state taking over the role of patriarch, creating a still more omnipresent Big Brother.

Nor is marriage the conjugal prison—the source of unending boredom, drudgery, and lovelessness—that "cool" know-nothing poseurs depict it to be. The truth is, a marriage is as exciting or boring as the two people who comprise it. A good marriage in fact protects against feelings of loneliness, and can give one's life focus. Had I not wasted mine chasing women nonstop, I could have been a contender, a somebody.

Still, of all social institutions, marriage—at least the traditional kind—is that of which the laws are the most difficult to follow, because they go against nature. Men are biologically more inclined than women to desire the opposite sex, and women, as guardians of hearth and home, are by nature more monogamous.

Asked how long the sexual connection ought to last, the poet Shelley said that a couple should stay together as long as they were united by love—and he meant only sexual love. He called it an intolerable tyranny if a man and a woman stayed together after the sexual attraction had worn off "and the most unworthy of toleration." I agree. Constancy has nothing virtuous in itself. The way to keep a good relationship going is for the man to fool around when he gets the urge, and to keep shtoom afterward. Never admit it and you will make the wife happy. Forget what she says. It's what you say that counts. And say nothing.

From the woman's perspective, the benefit of the bargain is that the rules are protective of the weak. We Greeks are used to keeping mistresses, but the wife and mother of our children remains the love of our life. She is a figure of respect, and it is understood that marriage is for life—a man does not turn in an old wife for a shiny new one, as if she were an automobile. Instead he has, as the French say, "an arrangement." As Gianni Agnelli, asked about his promiscuity, once put it on American television, "One can be a good husband and fool around just as one can be faithful and a bad one." The pussy-whipped American reporter was surprised. "What do you mean by that, John?"

The correct ratio of woman to man of course varies according to one's tastes and means. For me, the ideal at any given time is five to one. That is, in order for both parties to be happy and stay in love, a man should have five regular lovers. And I prefer variety where age is concerned. I like one girl who is nineteen, two who are twenty-four, one who is thirty-six, and, of course, my wonderful wife, at whatever age she is. Furthermore, a woman is much happier having one fifth of a good man, rather than having the whole of a lousy one.

What I truly do not understand are those Arab types who have harems consisting of five hundred women or so. Too impersonal. Like owning a candy store and munching away on chocolate all day and night. No, siree, five will do fine. This is the Taki fail-safe road to happiness and sexual well-being. Mind you, in a pinch, four will also do.

When the rules are understood and abided by, few womanizers ever divorce. Why should they? They are happy and so are their wives. They are not driven to adultery as a refuge, they have no need for affairs, for ego-boosting, or to avoid coming to grips with problems at home.

To be sure, there is the odd man who is made for monogamy. Paul Newman, long married to Joanne Woodward, once said of fooling around, "Why eat at McDonald's when you can have caviar at home?"

Closer to home, I had a friend who by appearances was a caricature of the ski-instructor-cum-seducer—fair, always tanned, with bright-blue eyes, a winning smile, and a very handsome face—and long ago, while he was training me for the winter Olympics, I could not but notice he drew girls around him like the proverbial turd draws flies. I quickly proposed to him a year-round association; he would accompany me everywhere, draw the girls, and leave the rest to me. But he let me down terribly. He had met a Scottish beauty and revealed to me that he was monogamous. It was a terrible waste and shame, but what can one do with unrelenting monogamous love? Despite my pleas, he married her and they've been happy and inseparable ever since.

On the plus side, it is not the worst thing when such competitors put themselves *hors de combat*. I once hurried across to the other side of the world to make sure that the bridegroom, the son of a friend, tied the knot, so to be put away for good. He had been moving into my territory for years, and it was only because of his father that I swallowed my pride and said nothing. I'm all for such men getting good and married.

Still, let's face it, monogamous men can be terrible bores, especially when they extol the virtues of their wives.

That said, I of course have taken the fatal step myself. Twice, in fact. And each time I knowingly threw caution to the wind.

There is an old calypso that says: "If you want to be happy for the rest of your life, never make a pretty woman your wife . . ."

Well, I beg to seriously differ. In my book, the prettier the woman the happier it makes me. *C'est tout*. Furthermore, a pretty woman keeps a man on his toes.

No beautiful woman will stay with a man who doesn't deserve her—not in the long run, anyway.

Suffice it to say that both times I married it was to a beauty.

Of course there were risks. Planning to be happy is always tricky, but that is especially so for the beautiful, because they live with exalted expectations. Beautiful people are supposed to be happy, and their endless quest for happiness can oftentimes make them miserable.

That may have been part of the problem the first time I took the plunge—not that I was wise enough at the time to give such things any thought.

I first saw the beautiful Cristina de Caraman on the July 1, 1961 cover of *Paris Match*, then in its heyday: "C'est une deb," announced the cover line, the once-upon-a-time annual British ritual having crossed the Channel to the land of cheese. The daughter of the Duke de Caraman, she was seventeen and so pretty and angelic-looking that even my mother, who was always after me to marry a Greek, told me she was the kind of girl I should get hold of rather permanently. I did that summer on the Riviera, where her mother's English family had a house high above Monte Carlo. Cristina's mother's maiden name was Macklin and her brother, Lance Macklin, was already a hero of mine, being a dare-devil racing driver back in the days when a crash meant instant fiery death.

I cannot remember having had a more idyllic time than I did that summer. And afterward, things continued as before. I was still on the tennis circuit (though with diminishing returns), and living the high life when out of sight of the prettiest girl in Paris.

It went on this way for about three years—too long for polite society—and finally Cristina gave me an ultimatum. She was about to turn twenty-one and was eager to leave her mother's house, since she couldn't stand climbing back through windows at the ungodliest hours of the morning any longer. "You either marry me or I can't see you any longer," came the threat. Cristina came from an old family full of tradition, and therefore used the traditional form of blackmail, none of this cheap "I'm pregnant" stuff.

I was about as eager to get married as I would later have been to have the Clintons to dinner, but, unlike them, Cristina was young and beautiful and charming. So like the Japanese after Nagasaki, I threw in the towel.

A big wedding was planned, which was not to my liking either.

The idea of signing away one's liberty in front of all those people seems almost obscene. Girls, however, cannot do without them, and I don't blame them. Winners traditionally celebrate their victories with a bash, and in front of as many witnesses as possible.

I asked for and was granted a three-month stay of execution so I could put my affairs in order. I then left Paris for New York to try and squeeze into three months what I was about to miss for the rest of my life. Fortuitously, both her parents and mine insisted that three thousand miles of water was the minimum distance that had to be kept between them and us.

Back in Paris, Cristina sent me sweet letters swearing undying love. But it is amazing how the impending loss of freedom can concentrate a man's mind on having fun. Before very long, I had the bad luck to meet an Anglo-American beauty going up a ski lift, and we were soon staying up until dawn seven nights a week, the all-American telling me how impressed she was with my habit of working at night in my father's shipping office. Of course, she was totally unaware that I was about to be married. And being the moral coward that I am, I remained quiet.

Then, as night follows day, it all came crashing down. Cristina flew to New York on a whim without telling me, and it was straight out of a cheap movie screenplay. The all-American—who was from the Midwest, and those girls don't take that kind of stuff sitting down—threw a pitcher of orange juice as I came into the Palace bar and called me a liar and a cheat in front of my bride, who proceeded to kick me on the shin as I've never been kicked before or since.

Cristina broke off our engagement and warned me that her father would shoot me if ever I came to Paris. (Don't forget, this was at a time when men were still supposed to act honorably, not like Neanderthals.) So I headed for Greece and the safety and comforts of home. My mother even suggested some mustachioed Greek girl as an excellent choice for a wife because she was definitely a virgin.

That was all I needed. I somehow managed to patch things up with Cristina.

Yet, incredibly—I suppose this goes to my state of mind—it happened again. When Cristina arrived in New York this time, on the eve of our wedding, and checked into the Sherry-Netherland Hotel, I was living there also—but on another floor, with a girl named Mimi.

Needless to say, I was extremely nervous, but still I was determined to have one last night of fun. So I told Cristina a story about a bachelor's party and how it was bad luck to see each other the day before the wedding, and went out with Mimi to El Morocco.

I had asked Rubi to be my best man, and he was at ElMo's that night also. Although far from an angel himself, he was appalled when he realized what was going on. In fact he ruined my last night of freedom with a lecture in front of Mimi. Mimi's last words to me were an embittered, "Did you really think that you could get away with it?"

But I did—almost. The next morning, January 10, 1965, a day that shall live in infamy, Rubi, Cristina, and I drove to Elizabeth, New Jersey, a town Frank Sinatra once accurately described as the armpit of the world. There I surrendered unconditionally before a federal judge, who stopped handing out life terms long enough to declare me and Cristina man and wife. (There was a major Mafia trial going on at the time; everyone got off but me, and ten years later the judge was indicted for corruption.)

All well and good. Except when we got back to the hotel, I knew I had made a major miscalculation. Mimi was waiting in the lobby. She came up and sweetly asked my bride whether we had just been married. When she heard the word yes, again I got kicked in the shin, and she walked away.

On that note, our married life began. And of course she never really trusted me again.

For this, I take my full share of responsibility. Despite her great beauty and impeccable background, she was jealous, and I guess I'd forgotten to tell her about my theories. No sooner would I start flirting with someone than my wife would hurl insults at her. Worse, she would sometimes flirt herself in retaliation, and that was simply not acceptable according to my rules.

Most of our altercations took place in restaurants and nightclubs, where we amused and entertained the jet set and not a small number of waiters and busboys. We were a perfect match, like the proverbial terrorist and hand grenade. Needless to say, her jealousy provoked me to do things that later interfered with my pursuit of the good life. Such as always being assigned a hotel room on street level after it became known that I had thrown her luggage out of a top floor hotel room and narrowly missed killing the Swiss president.

In retrospect, the marriage was on the rocks from the start. Still, for the next three years, between battles, we partied nonstop, attending every chic ball in Paris, London, and the Riviera, never staying in a place long enough to collect the laundry—it was done by hand in those halcyon days.

Our living arrangements were congenial. My wife lived at home, on avenue Raymond Poincaré, with her mother, her dog, and her nanny, and I lived in a small suite at the Plaza Athénée. The reason for this was simple. Both Cristina and I were very independent and were convinced that if we lived together immediately it would traumatize us to such an extent that our marriage would fail. And we had good reasons for not wanting that to happen. Everyone, including her father—a man known never to be right about anything—had predicted that it wouldn't last a year. My ambition was to have my cake and eat it too; hers was to prove her father wrong yet again.

Needless to say, the arrangement suited me perfectly. The Plaza Athénée was a great place in those days. There were no Arabs, except for the ones who swept up the Relais after it closed at 2 a.m., and the manager would make an exception for a young couple where prices were concerned, an unheard of phenomenon today.

Also Madame Claude's (and the Sixties were Claude's best years) was situated a mere quarter of a mile away, on the rue Marignan. I used Claude's place quite a lot that year because I was under tremendous pressure from my father. I had convinced him that a tennis mad public would tear him apart if he forced me to leave the circuit and go to work. He had believed it for nine years, but by 1965 he was starting to doubt my veracity. "Do something in the French Championships or the honeymoon is over," he had warned me, and little did he guess how prophetic his words were.

As everyone who has been under pressure knows, nothing relieves it better than a visit to a brothel. And as luck would have it—bad luck, that is—my Greek doubles partner and I drew the top seeded American team in the first round of the French Championships that year.

The day of the match I decided to lunch in my suite in order to concentrate. My wife decided to lend her support and showed up for company. We didn't have too many things to talk about in those days, so she brought along her best friend, Denise Shorto.

Denise was beautiful then, so I didn't mind the interruption. What I did mind as I brooded about my rotten luck in the draw was her and Cristina's topic of conversation, which was all about who was rich and who was not. No one, not even a gossip columnist, had ever accused either of them of being an intellectual, but now, being under tremendous pressure, their chatter prompted me to do something rather juvenile. I sprayed the two girls with my soup and laughed sophomorically. Cristina went bonkers. She always had a terrible temper and I should have known better. She grabbed a large plate and threw it with all her might toward me. From two feet away. I blocked it but it cut a deep gash on my arm.

Blood squirted out like Saudi oil and the girls began to scream and feel faint.

I, on the other hand, was relieved. I had my excuse for playing badly. When the doctor arrived he asked me how it happened.

"Well, doc," I told him, "one of those girls is my wife, the other my mistress, and they finally got smart."

"Ah, monsieur, vous êtes un homme formidable!" the doctor responded, deeply impressed.

That afternoon, relaxed in the knowledge that I had a perfect excuse, Nick Kalo and I had two match points against the Americans, Ralston and Richey, but I managed to lose them both. When I got back to the hotel the doctor had left a message asking me to dinner any time that week. Bring your friends, it said.

Of course, in the end her father this once was proven right. Cristina finally decided that my womanizing was not conducive to a stable marriage and children. Deciding she had had enough, and that life would be more fun without me, she flew off to Brazil where Denise was marrying Baron Thyssen, Europe's richest man.

For me, as for much of the world, the year of 1968 was an *annus horribilis*. My mistress told me she would no longer put up with the humiliation of taking second place to my wife. Then my father became angry with me for doing nothing but chase women. And now my wife!

I was in despair. Like all Greeks, I threatened to kill her and any man who came near her. Like all Greeks, of course, I did nothing of the sort.

Nevertheless, I moped for weeks, boring everyone with stories of impending suicide. Though the thought actually never crossed my mind, my mother fell for it, and soon my father came to the rescue, telephoning me in Paris. "Your mother is worried about you," he said, "though I know you are faking." Nonetheless, he told me I could go and buy myself a boat and charge it to him.

My only regret after accepting my father's generous offer was that I had not thought of threatening suicide before. As an old salt once said, "He who has a boat can have a different wife every night."

Do I regret the marriage? Of course not—I chalk it up to experience. The way it unfolded was nobody's fault. We were both young and ill-formed. We came into the marriage with radically different expectations on key matters, so it was impossible we would ever see eye to eye.

I remember a conversation I had the year before it ended with Gaston Palewski, a close associate of de Gaulle's. As randy as they come, he'd invited us to the Elysée Palace because he had his eye on Cristina. During lunch, he'd tried to play footsie, but she told him to lay off.

Afterward, I commiserated with him.

"These young people are unaware of the old customs, monsieur . . ."

EIGHTEEN

Surviving the Fatal Plunge

MY SECOND humiliation took place in New York City, on March 5, 1981. Alexandra insisted we get married in order for our children to have a chance of getting into a good school. For some strange reason Americans insist that parents should be married, a middle-class attitude to say the least. I tried to keep it as quiet as possible, as I was working on certain projects at the time. So I arranged for yet another federal judge to come down to my father's lawyers' office and perform the deed.

Afterward I asked for one month's leave in order to recover from the ordeal, and the mother of my children, Princess Alexandra Schoenburg-Hartenstein, very kindly granted it.

It was in large part her extremely mature approach to life that had drawn me to Alexandra in the first place. Yes, she was beautiful and intelligent, and a marvel on the slopes. Still, the key moment may have been her reaction to a sticky situation soon after we met, one that under other circumstances might have been disastrous. After the end of my first marriage I was living in both London and Athens and had developed a serious liaison in each place. Alexandra, meanwhile, was living in Paris. I used to visit her as often as I could, but of course refrained from revealing what I was doing when I was elsewhere. What mattered was that I was kind and considerate whenever I was with her. As long as I withheld that I was living with others, everything was perfect. Then my Greek girlfriend got ideas, and everybody ended up in tears. After which, the English girlfriend I'd been seeing at the same time called Alexandra and offered a full confession. Alexandra's reaction? She said she could bear anything except that.

Now there was a woman!

Byron, ever the romantic, but also a legendary cynic, said, "All tragedies are finished by a death, all comedies ended by a marriage . . ." Not true! Ours is a very happy marriage, and it has produced two wonderful children. It is grounded, as every good relationship must be, in shared values and common understandings, and one of these is that my wife sits at home Penelope-like, while I can run around as long as I remain discreet.

Indeed, my wife understood implicitly that if you are hitched to a womanizer, demanding the truth on matters of fidelity leads to an unhealthy marriage. Further, she knows that the healthy adulterer can carry on an affair without destroying his marriage, that he is non-demanding and non-compulsive, and that he will never use an adulterous affair to ignore problems in his home life. To the contrary, whenever I am having an affair, she tells me how kind, tolerant, and sensitive to her needs I am. Which makes sense. Unhealthy adulterers—those who are driven to have affairs as a refuge or an ego boost, are hostile to their wives, the opposite of a romantic womanizer. All of which is to say, it's been a smooth ride from the start.

Okay, no, there have been a few ashtrays thrown at me over the years, and the occasional harsh word. But what Alexandra has never been without is perspective, and just as importantly, a sense of humor. I recall the time, soon after we began living together, that she accused me of having an affair. I swore to her that the relationship in question was strictly platonic, and that God should strike me dead if it was not. As I said it, I collapsed with a thud on the parquet floor. She did not fall for it, but she burst out laughing.

Not long ago I met a pretty girl on Hertford Street, and when I asked her to put her number into my phone, she noticed a picture of yours truly with the mother of my children and our two kids. "Who is that, your wife?" she inquired. "It's the nanny," said I, and then swallowed hard when she replied that my children looked rather grown-up to still have a nanny.

And when I told Alexandra later, again she laughed.

None of this is to suggest she doesn't suffer from some of the characteristic feminine impulses. But regarded in the right light, even these can be a kind of blessing. Women act illogically in order to make their man act like one—clear-cut, decisive, self-directing. Femininity needs masculinity.

Example. Early on in our relationship, before she had yet produced any offspring, we were not getting along well, and she started seeing a shrink. When I found out I flew into a rage. "No wonder you're crazy and paranoid," I told her. "A shrink will do it quicker than a Soviet asylum!"

Being a woman, she thought she could convince me by making me meet her guru. I agreed, knowing full-well that the shrink who could stand up to my basic common sense had not as yet been conceived. When I entered her office—yes, she was a woman—she took one look at me and collapsed. I assumed this was normal until the future mother of my children explained to me that the doctor was suffering from kidney stones. When the poor woman recovered, she began interrogating me about what I liked in life. When I blurted out that I had never seen an attractive woman whom I didn't feel like going to bed with—in other words, the truth—she let out a horrible scream and collapsed again.

She insisted that it was a kidney stone passing through, but I knew better. More to the point, la Schoenburg was confirmed in the view that it was indeed best to accept the truth about nature and man, and not probe too deeply in search of trouble.

The fact is, the current mania for confession is disastrous, not only for countless private lives, but for society at large. We may hurt ourselves with our sins, but with our confessions, we only hurt others.

As far as I'm concerned, admitting to an affair is for mean people. It used to be that when a man told a lover or a wife what he did with another it was called cruelty; now it's called sincerity or, even more laughably, kindness. The truth is, confession has needlessly broken up innumerable happy relationships.

Group therapy—invented in America naturally—has played an especially sinister role in encouraging the sharing of feelings. It has by now evolved into a kind of demon principle that one should be open to everybody. Under the advice of some quack, reasonable people confess to complete strangers to having been naughty—unlike sensible Roman Catholics, who confess to ones they can't actually see. The result is entirely predictable: even more broken relationships. Why? Because people don't change. For all the ballyhoo about the sexual liberation of the Sixties, it did nothing to lessen normal human reactions, starting with the pain of jealousy. Personally, I'd rather spend a day being quizzed by the Gestapo than take part in such a humiliating process.

Under the regime of therapists, America has become a jungle of screaming women and angry men. Unsolicited and tediously long-winded details about someone's sex life can drive most people to drugs. In America, people spill the beans about their most intimate details even when not on drugs.

And lately it has moved on to the next stage. Everyone not only feels wounded, but entitled to feel offended by anything anyone else says.

What's been lost in all this is skill at small talk, which long-served a vital cultural function, in that it was devised by the wise to enable people to escape such self-absorbed bores. Taki's advice to the young and not-so-young: Never share, never admit, never bore, and everything will be hunky-dory.

Still, in even the happiest of homes . . .

Which is to say, we did have one genuine moment of crisis. It was in the winter of 1985, and I had been behaving badly, being more overt than necessary, and my darling Alexandra was hinting that she'd had enough. As a warning she had taken the children from our home in New York to her mother's in Paris. At the same time, an English friend of mine in London had run off with yet another friend, a male who looked exactly like a pig, thus making it obvious that I was about to lose both a wife and a mistress. More catastrophically still, an English woman in New York was dropping hints about having a child—false ones as it turned out, but about as welcome at that point in my life as would be even more lawbreakers streaming across the Mexican border nowadays.

How lost was I at that moment, without the mother of my children?

This will provide some indication.

Needing to be alone to think, I went for dinner at Mortimer's, a chic watering hole, now defunct, three blocks from my house on the Upper East Side. I had had a couple of bottles of wine and was starting to relax when André Leon Talley, a very tall and talented African American who worked for *Vogue*, known to us as the "African Queen," came into the place accompanied by a beautiful, and almost as tall, lady.

The place was jammed so I waved them over and they sat down to dinner with lonely old me. Her name was Iman, and she had recently arrived in the States having been discovered in deepest Africa by my good buddy Peter Beard, the photographer. To call it a convivial dinner would be an understatement. I was in my cups and my guests were laughing at my predicament. I invited them over to my house for a drink but André had to work early and begged off. Iman agreed to one drink. We walked over to my house, but when we got there I realized to my horror that in my distress I had not taken my keys with me. Worse, I had told the live-in help to take the night off as I had not planned to go out. The terror mounted after I failed to break the door down by kicking hard on the lock. As I became more and more desperate, Iman started to get scared. I found a crowbar nearby and began to chop away at the damn door, whereupon she ran off and jumped into a passing taxi. Just then the door gave in. There I was with a door I could not shut—the crime rate was still very high in New York in those days—and no Iman. The poor little Greek boy never had it so bad.

Around the same time, I went to Montreal for a wedding. It was held at the incredible home of the billionaire philanthropist Jackie Desmarais, who was one of the best women I've ever met. I told her I was rather down because both my mistress and my wife were about to dump me. "That would be a catastrophe," said Jackie simply. "Put all your efforts into saving the wife."

The best advice ever from a very wise lady.

That's what I did, and it's been relatively smooth sailing all the years since. I often ask Alexandra when she complains about my behavior whether she would prefer me to be a lousy husband and a faithful one, or the opposite. She lies and says the former, though usually with a smile.

Okay, she did threaten to leave me when I was in Pentonville—but what could be more understandable?—and happily she soon thought better of it.

The only serious pain I've inflicted on her since that terrible time was the physical kind, and accidentally of course. We were on the slopes and—because of age, bravado, and the refusal to accept that things ain't what they used to be—I was skiing out of control. And though I have been a very bad boy most of my life, the one time I wish Alexandra had not turned a blind eye, she did. She was standing still in front of a mogul when I made a sharp left turn and crashed into her at full speed. As I knocked her down, my skis ran over her face crushing her nose and causing two deep gashes on her forehead. I then rolled down the mountain unable to stop because of the horrendous plastic garments we now wear that accelerate our speed on snow. I went down the slope about a quarter of a mile before I stopped, relatively unharmed. My son-in-law and daughter meanwhile came to my wife's aid. She was bleeding a lot but, following a helicopter ride to Bern and X-rays, it was revealed her perfect nose was very bruised but not broken. Still, within a day she looked like she'd gone five rounds with Mike Tyson at his peak—large gashes, both eyes deep purple and black. Even thinking of it now, I am horrified.

There you have it: Life is about what we can and cannot control. Fortunately on this occasion, everything ended up hunky-dory, except she didn't look so good, and for a time she was out of action, having to cancel her social engagements until further notice.

But there were insights to be gleaned. For one thing, I had to consider that it was perhaps time to slow down and grow up. Besides that, I considered the vagaries of life, all the awful people I'd rather have crashed into—do Bill and Hillary ski? Yet above all, the near-tragedy served as a reminder that Alexandra is the person in the world I cherish more than any other. More than fifty years is a long time to be Madame Taki.

So I do recognize how lucky I am. Few wives are as good-humored as mine—a fact of which I am reminded all the time.

There is, for instance, the wife of Charlie, the driver at our home in Gstaad. Charlie is as fond of women as any other man but, like so many women, his wife continually seeks to impose herself on the natural order of things. When I once made the mistake of joking to Charlie's wife about all the hookers who know him by his first name while he waits for me outside the station in Wengen, you'd think I'd given her evidence her spouse was a serial killer with a specialty in pedophilia.

Poor Charlie. When once he noticed a pretty French maid in my kitchen and commented he found her attractive, I replied: "As she does you."

That got him all agitated and he asked what I based that on. "She commented how attractive you are for a mature man," I told him. "And what did you say to her?" said Charlie. "Well, I told her that, yes, lots of women find you attractive, but you were true to your wife and never strayed as you are 100 percent homosexual."

Charlie fell for my tale and lost it, gesticulating so wildly he almost drove off the road. "It's for your own sake," I assured him. "I don't want you to have any more trouble with your wife."

With Princess Schoenburg things couldn't be more different. The last time I returned to Gstaad after an extended stay in New York, she came on to the driveway to greet me as Charlie delivered the sleepy Greek boy home. I pretended not to know her and embraced the maid instead. My son and two grandchildren added to the merriment, playing along when I asked them who that lady was who tried to kiss me. And Alexandra laughed right along.

In all the years we've been married, and although she's never been exactly pleased with my fooling around, my wife has never embarrassed me in public, except for once. We were going to some premiere in New York and some hack asked me the name of the lady I was with. "She's the mother of my children," said I.

"That's what he thinks," trilled Alexandra.

NINETEEN

The Right Friends, and Life Is a Holiday

When I got busted on July 23, 1984 and was sent to prison, I did not lose a single friend. Not one.

It is one of the things I'm most proud of in my misspent life.

The night before I was to enter Pentonville my friends David Tang and John Aspinall gave a dinner for me. Everyone got up and said a few words about how awful it was that the poor little Greek boy had to go down. No one thought of saying I got what I deserved. My lefty friend Alexander Chancellor was in especially good form—ever eager to stick the knife in, he blamed Mrs. Thatcher's fascist government. It was that type of evening.

When it was Jeff Bernard's turn, my old *Spectator* colleague rose and told a very complicated story about a guy asking some bimbo if he could perform oral sex on her. She finally agrees and while he's at it he reads *The Mill on the Floss*. When he finished someone asked Jeff what this had to do with me going to prison, and he acted genuinely surprised. "What, Taki is going to prison?"

Six months later, when I got out, I was surprised to be met by another old pal, Nigel Dempster. When I'd first been arrested it was Nigel, along with Charles Benson, my oldest English buddy, who'd been the first to come to my rescue. Benson arrived with a posh lawyer who supposedly could reduce a murder charge to a traffic violation. Like a fool, I instead chose a local Indian chap who convinced me that posh lawyers were the wrong mouthpieces for drug cases. During my time in lockup, Benson never allowed me to forget, nor did his posh lawyer friend.

But now Nigel came alone, since Benson was in bad shape and confined to hospital, and in a pelting rain, that is where Nigel drove me. Nigel went into his room first and told Benson that he had gone to Heathrow to pick me up, but that I had been again arrested for drugs and had gone straight to the cells.

"Oh no, that stupid Greek will never learn," croaked Bens.

When it was my turn to enter, I told Charles that the fuzz had allowed me to go free because I said I'd be visiting the greatest man of the English turf. That got a laugh out of my old friend. But then it all became a bit too much for me. What a bummer.

Without Benson there was no way I'd go again to Ascot—it would have been like going to Windsor Castle and discovering Tony and Cherie Blair living there.

While Benson had gotten out of lots of tricky situations over the years, it was clear there would be no miracle this time. It was a severe blow.

It is hard to adequately describe the role my friends have played in my life. I will only say I have been privileged to have known some of the best men of my time. Though they may have differed in superficial respects—sometimes, if very occasionally, even politically—all have been of a certain stripe. They belong to a brotherhood defined by strongly held attitudes—about women, and the definition of the good life—and a keen sense of honor. We might at times have been competitors, even the fiercest of rivals. Yet when the chips were down, we've always known we were there for one another.

And, always, with them, there were joyous times.

Take for instance, Yanni Zographos. Having been born with a platinum spoon in his mouth, he was not into the work ethic, yet he dispensed personal and emotional wealth everywhere he went. Everyone went to him with their problems, and needless to say, a long line of freeloaders, stock brokers, out of luck gamblers, and gold mine speculators followed him everywhere. But his kindnesses to me were many and heartfelt.

One evening in the summer of 1957, a very sad young Taki was at the roulette table nearest to the bar in the Monte Carlo sporting club, having already lost his monthly allowance after one hour of gambling. Yanni was sternly lecturing me about the evils of gambling—though between lectures, he himself was also punting rather heavily. Sitting nearby, Sir Winston Churchill wasn't having much luck either, despite the fact that the croupiers were desperately trying to make his numbers come up.

Suddenly, Sir Winnie's luck changed. The old boy hit ten numbers in a row. Nothing to do with luck, of course. In a twist on Rick in *Casablanca*, Ari Onassis, who owned the place, had simply ordered the croupiers to place the Churchill chips on the numbers after they had come up. Sir Winston was delighted as he was none the wiser. On his last bet, as the croupiers were about to pay out the "lucky" winner, Yanni looked at my forlorn expression and announced, pointing at yours truly, "Alors, il faut aussi payer le petit." Onassis looked up, guffawed, then burst out laughing, and said in Greek, "I'll let it go this time because your young friend looks so miserable."

It may well have been the only dishonest thing Yanni ever did in his life. And of course, he had done it for me.

But, then, he was my guardian angel. Not very long afterward, he proved an even greater benefactor on the amorous front.

At the time I was still a struggling player on the tennis circuit, and after a heartbreaking loss in Deauville, I decided I'd finally had enough.

I retreated to the Riviera, having convinced myself that the solution to my troubles lay in the fabled land of Fitzgerald.

Until then I had only been there before with my parents, but Yanni was there, holding court at the Hôtel du Cap, so I knew I was in good hands. Sure enough, when I arrived he'd reserved a room for me at the Carlton in Cannes—room 303. Then, for my first night on the town he took me to the casino. Unfortunately, I had a fever as a result of a bad cold; the temperature and the nonstop drinks were a bad mix, so I was feeling out of sorts.

Until, that is, I spotted the current girl of my dreams, the chanteuse Juliette Gréco!

She was across the casino with her boyfriend, the one-time head of 20th Century Fox, Darryl F. Zanuck. I knew the story—that Zanuck had fallen hard when he saw her perform in a Parisian Left Bank bistro and decided to make her a film star. They were on the Riviera to cast *The Roots of Heaven*, the movie that would be her introduction, and I was led to understand that every night Zanuck gambled very large sums at the chemmy table, while Juliette sat next to him playing every hand with much smaller sums.

As I watched Juliette and Darryl gambling, I imagined that she looked at me and smiled. And before leaving for my hotel, still feeling very much out of sorts, I informed Yanni of the fact.

I fell asleep as soon as my head hit the pillow, but was awoken abruptly when my door opened. A woman came in. "It's me, Juliette. Do not turn on the light," she whispered.

She quickly undressed and slithered naked under the sheets.

Everything I'd ever read or imagined about the south of France went racing through my befogged mind. But what I hadn't expected were the howls that Juliette let out as we began our love-making. Shutters banged and lights were turned on as her screams echoed around the cavernous courtyard. Things quieted down rather quickly after that—I was, after all, not yet twenty-one—and she dressed hurriedly, kissed me goodnight, and left in the dark.

My only thought as I went to sleep: What a way to start my stay on the French Riviera!

Youth is not characterized by discretion, and in the morning I told Yanni. He congratulated me, as did Julien, the fabled concierge of the Carlton, who controlled everything and was the most important person to know on the Riviera.

That evening, feeling better but still with a fever, I returned to the casino with Yanni after a sumptuous dinner and lots of champagne on the terrace of the Carlton. Darryl and Juliette were at their usual table punting away. I caught her eye and gave her a big smile but she did not respond. I figured it was just the cynical sexual reality of the Riviera, a baptism of fire so to speak.

Unbelievably, my door opened again at around 4:30 that morning and Juliette Gréco came in silently, undressed, and got into bed with me. This time her love-making shrieks prompted a fellow guest to announce: "Ça recommence."

She followed the same procedure and left after a brief, wordless kiss in the dark.

The next morning, I packed to move on to Antibes, and told Yanni over the telephone that as Zanuck had a cabana next to his, I would bring things to a head where Juliette was concerned. "I've had it with this bullshit. If I'm good enough to sleep with . . ." Yanni didn't say a word. As I paid my small bill, Julien took me aside. Looking like a wise uncle, he advised me not to make a fuss because Zanuck was a very jealous man. "And, after all, it wasn't Mademoiselle Gréco who visited you these past two nights but a popular streetwalker known as "The Screamer." It was Monsieur

Zographos's idea—I just chose the lady of the night. She looks like Gréco, n'est-ce pas?"

As far as jokes go, this one was brilliant. I fell for it and then some.

Every time I saw Juliette on screen after that, I felt cheated somehow.

In 1982, Yanni married and our travels together ceased. We remained just as close, but he stopped hunting for women. When he fell ill, it was very hard to see him wasting away. Toward the end, uncomplaining as ever, he would cry when I came to see him and tell me how much he loved me. He cried because he was losing me, not the other way round.

When he died, it was the first time I had broken down since my father's death. He was, after all, like my dad, always protecting me. He left behind his wife, his ten-year-old boy, and his saint of a sister. He lived his life unconcerned about its meaning, yet he was never unconcerned about his fellow man. As we Greeks say, "May the earth that covers you be soft."

I am not in general a sentimental man, but such losses were very hard. Rubi, my mentor, also went far too young. Once upon a time gigolos were he-men, and Rubirosa was the ideal of the type. Rubi spent the money he earned in the bedroom and on the good things in life, mostly other women, strings of polo ponies, and two very nice houses in France. But in every case, when it was ended, it was over—nothing so vulgar as going to court over money. All his exes loved him not just because he was a tiger in the bedroom and a hell of an athlete outside it, but because he treated them with respect and was very romantic to boot. It was their pleasure to willingly shower him with presents. Barbara Hutton bought him seventeen polo ponies. Doris Duke gave him a B-17, which he flew without knowing how to navigate by asking friends like me to follow the railroad lines from Deauville to Paris. He was also a racing driver, a great polo player, a tough boxer, and Taki's best man.

Guts? When the Dominican strongman Rafael Trujillo was assassinated back in the early 1960s—the old boy died with his boots on, having had a quickie with his young Pepita just before he was ambushed, later emerging from his car mortally wounded to shoot one of his assassins—Rubirosa immediately chartered a Boeing 707 to fly the dictator's two sons and himself to Ciudad Trujillo to save the regime. (I always liked the idea that Trujillo had called the capital after himself.) But he later told me with disgust that it had been a waste, since the two sons were soft and did not want to crack heads. Unsurprisingly, they ended up as playboys in Spain.

I was with Rubi at New Jimmy's in Montparnasse until 3 a.m. on July 6, 1965, celebrating a polo victory, and only left because I had to be on court for a tournament in Nice the next morning. (That's how we trained back then: in nightclubs doing a fast mambo.) Rubi left Jimmy's shortly after six, drove through a deserted Paris on his way home across the Pont de Saint-Cloud and into the Bois de Boulogne. As an ex-racing driver—Le Mans, Sebring, and a one-off in a Formula 1—Rubi was going much too fast. He clipped the back of a parked car, and when his steering jammed ran straight into a tree, dying instantaneously. A newspaper wrote the next day: "Had he been wearing his seat belt nothing would have happened to him." Perhaps. But if he had put on his belt, he would not have been Porfirio Rubirosa.

For such friends, we will do almost anything. They are loyal and trustworthy and make life endlessly pleasurable. My pal Jeff Jansz, who married nine of the 900 women he seduced, was once married to a South African girl who one day informed him that she might have caught a bad social disease. Jeff, obviously no angel, was certain he must have infected his wife, and therefore was understanding and took her directly to her gynecologist. No sooner had the gyno been told the news than Jeff saw him running into his private office and injecting himself with penicillin.

You can guess the rest. The marriage broke up, and some time later Jeff arrived to visit me in Mykonos where I was in training with the Greek karate team. Upon landing, the first person he saw was the gyno with his ex-wife and a crowd of South African friends. Words were exchanged, and then five of us took on about twenty of them, for Jeff's sake.

We'd all been there, more or less, and as they say, it was the least one could do.

The years, with all their ups and downs, ought to teach us caution. But my friend Tim Hoare was one who remained reckless to the end. He was generous to a fault, extremely intelligent, and well-read. His words, in vintage 1940s posh English tones, would tumble out so fast, enwrapped in alliteration and so clogged with onomatopoeia, that the poor little Greek boy would miss three out of every four. But what stood out was his fearlessness and grace under pressure. Once Tim's private plane blew an engine mid-flight and was circling uncontrollably. He was alone with the two panicked pilots. But when he rang me up, he failed to so much as mention the trouble, merely saying that he might be a while.

Tim never lost touch with the overflowing joy and curiosity of the young. And, like the young, he remained confident of the future despite the degradation of our culture. At his funeral, his son Harry spoke of how as a little boy he had spotted some scars on Tim's stomach and asked about them. Tim said they were from a fight with a lion. It then became a fight with a leopard. Only when Harry grew up did he realize that they were stretch marks. This was classic Tim.

But so too was that, nearing the end, he made a point of expressing love to all his friends and thanking us individually for a life of happiness. Whatever sorrow he may have felt about his upcoming death he kept to himself. That is what courage and grace are all about.

At my current age, it is more and more like an Agatha Christie mystery, with the question being, Who's next? My wonderful merry band of Pugs are mainly in our eighties. Yet it is not fear of leaving that is the problem. It is missing those who have left us.

TWENTY

The Alpha Male at Rest

THE MAN on the other end of the telephone did not ask me anything embarrassing. All he wanted to know was if women still come on to an oldie, or are they a thing of the past? In short, have women abandoned a sinking ship?

I do have a certain sense of decorum, so know how ridiculous a man my age can sound when talking about women, especially younger women. I have been chasing beautiful women all my life and will likely continue to do so until the moment the man in the white suit pays me a visit.

But there is also reality, and it is pretty straightforward: There is nothing better than youth, and, no, it is not wasted on the young. Not in the important ways. Everything works, injuries disappear after a night's sleep, one's too busy to notice the stupidity of others, too intolerant of weakness to acknowledge one's own. Even a broken heart mends at the sight of someone new.

Most important of all is that youth lacks a timetable. Tomorrow really never comes.

Now in my mid-eighties, by every standard I am in excellent physical shape because I work at it. Take it from Taki: All you need to feel good and able to enjoy yourself is a little exercise before breakfast, and some semi-hard training in the afternoon. *C'est tout, mes amis.*

So how should an oldie start the day? Whether or not with a hangover, by stretching. After a couple of minutes of that, two minutes on a stationary bike, full tilt. This gets the heart rate up. Then forty pushups, twenty with the hands close together, twenty more with hands apart.

Isometrics follow, pushing against a wall while standing, followed by sitting against a wall on an imaginary stool for one minute. Then it's front kicks and reverse punches for speed and accuracy using a bag and a makiwara. In the afternoon, a session of kickboxing or karate and a brisk walk before dinner leave you ready for anything the night might offer.

Except what is THAT?

The ancient Greeks famously revered old age. But they got old in their late twenties. A man of eighty in old Athens would be a 250-year-old in today's world.

And forget that stuff about salt-and-pepper hair being taken for wisdom—an old man started that rumor, along with the one about how long men remain fertile, and how in men wrinkles lend gravitas, and how much more tolerant older men are and less given to drama. Never mind, we all know what girls think of 250-year-old men. Not much. In my travels I have yet to meet an extremely intelligent girl who preferred older men to younger ones.

And speaking of big lies, I was told sixty and seventy years ago that if I reached a ripe old age, the rage to live would subside and an inner peace would take hold of me. It's as big a lie as socialism, or the one that says we're all created equal.

And here's one more truism, courtesy of George Herbert: "He that is not handsome at twenty, nor strong at thirty, nor rich at forty, nor wise at fifty, will never be handsome, strong, rich, or wise."

It is not easy to accept. I have been a sportsman at the highest levels, as well as a lifelong pursuer of the fairer sex, and I know how similar are the waning days of each—that is, how potent is the temptation for self-delusion. Fate tends to play cruel tricks by sending confusing signals. A lucky punch or a perfectly run pass pattern can delude the aging jock into thinking the old magic is still there—and it usually takes a coach or manager to tell him the painful truth. But there is no one to tell an aging seducer his time is up. An exceptional party, a sudden unexpected conquest, even a particularly enjoyable stay at the right resort can fool one into staying on the merry-go-round one more season, inevitably with catastrophic results.

Of course, those who complain about old age are silly and very boring. To be happy when old one needs luck and good health, and I have both. One weighs up the few triumphs and disasters, the ethical choices one has or has not made. Yet one also appreciates the happiness that comes from small pleasures, such as violent karate training, stolen kisses, family evenings, and boozing with friends. Travel is no longer a must, especially when one has been almost everywhere and seen almost everything there is to see.

Throughout my life I've looked for action and thrills, and now all of a sudden I'm content to sit in my garden, look at the incredible, straight-out-of-*The-Sound-of-Music* mountain views, and be very happy. It is, of course, a bit of a shame, the end of an era and all that, but it happens to everyone, anyone, that is, who survives past his sixties.

According to Cicero, and I agree with him, character is very important in old age. Once I would have described happiness from within as going to bed alone and finding Ava Gardner under the covers; now it means recalling such a thing and smiling at the Taki I was.

There is a lot of this—nostalgia that is, for time wasted that was well lived nonetheless. I recently saw a picture, circa 1959, of Coco Chanel surrounded by eight of her beautiful models. I knew all of them except for Mademoiselle Chanel, as they all called her, and two of them had been very grand love affairs. Seeing the picture brought a kind of pain only sensitive souls like the poor little Greek boy can feel. But it also reminded me that mine were the two prettiest by far. Indeed, in a city renowned for its beauties, both ladies were known as the most beautiful, each having that nonchalant grace few American women are known for. Those two affairs took place four years apart, in 1959 and 1963, when I was twenty-three and twenty-seven, they were twenty-five and twenty-eight. I later learned that Chanel advised both of her girls to marry me—Greeks are good fathers and love their children, she told them. Also, of course, she'd asked if I had money, and both had answered that I did not but my father did, and that was good enough.

Gazing at that old photograph, I wondered if those ethereal creatures were still alive and, more, hoped against hope that they had managed to retain their beauty into old age.

Not long ago I dreamt of a girl I met even earlier, in the summer of 1953, in Greece. We spent two months together and had a platonic love affair. She was older than me, but not by much. I had turned sixteen that summer and had been to bed with a couple of "nice" girls by then, but the rest had been mostly hookers. Her name was Maria Agapitou, and she was a rare beauty, at least in my inexperienced eyes. We first met in a park in a northern resort of Athens, where I was sitting on a bench reading *Tender Is the Night*. She noticed, and said in perfect English that the book would inspire me to lead a dissolute life. "I sure hope so," I answered. That did it. We started to meet every day in that beautiful jasmine-scented park among the pines. She was taller than me by an inch, had light brown curly hair and blue eyes, and would be described as pre-Raphaelite, a term I didn't know existed then. She also spoke beautifully, in a language I wasn't used to, using torrents of adjectives when talking about literature, and in sensuous phrases that left me thinking about them long after she and I had parted.

We went to the flicks, as we called them, in an outdoor cinema, where she caught me looking at her sideways and told me to look at the screen. I also tried to hold hands right away, but she pulled hers away.

Most of the time she wore a black dress, but one day she wore white at a party given by some friend. She knew everyone there, a crowd aged mostly twenty and over. "I see you brought your *Americanaki,*" said the hostess. The little American. No one bothered to speak to me so I proceeded to get very drunk, so drunk that I had to lie down on a sofa near the entrance where I passed out.

We didn't see each other for some time after that—I didn't dare go to the park—but then she walked into my life once again as I sat pretending to read. Maria would reject every pass I made. I would say nothing but would hide for a couple of days hoping against hope that my disappearance would make her change her mind, and then the saga would start all over again.

Young love can be as traumatic as hell, and I was really traumatized. All I did was think about her. I stopped playing tennis, stopped going to the brothels, stopped seeing my friends. There's nothing like unrequited love to drive one over the top.

But was it unrequited? All these years later I can remember perfectly the look she used to give me.

The end was too painful to recall. One moment I was talking to her and shyly trying to avoid her gaze, the next I was heading back to school. I did not take her address or write to her. But over Christmas my mother told me that she had gotten married. Then, the following spring, I heard that she had died.

Was it true that she had gotten married, and then died? I should have realized what a moral coward I was that I never tried to find out. Was it my mother's way of making me forget about her? Could she still be alive?

That time is the flickering ecstasy of a long-ago memory, and the impression that a young woman made on a teenager, and an inner voice tells me to beware of nostalgia. After all, I last saw her more than six decades ago.

But I still dream about her.

Of course, there's also the other kind of nostalgia, the one for the kind of world I grew up in. Not just the nightclubs or even the innocence, but for the assumptions about right and wrong and good and bad. If freedom of speech was a capital offense in Germany in 1940, political correctness makes it very nearly as rare in London and New York today. In fact, the stifling culture of woke makes the sacrifices of those young men who fell in Normandy seem, if not exactly in vain, a kind of crude mockery. The material and spiritual degradation of the post-modern West—the porn, the violence, and the greed—are not worth the life of a single G.I. Call me a cynic if you like, but after visiting the graves of young Americans, British, Canadian, and German soldiers, grief was replaced by rage at how we've squandered our precious victory. We are now prisoners of a stifling cultural uniformity that quickly and mercilessly punishes those who trespass. Qualities such as virtue and civility are seen as not only irrational, but as actually harmful. We live in a time where humbug reigns supreme.

But the great compensation is in family. The definition of serendipity is finding a needle in a haystack. Well, I found mine far from the haystack, on the Right Bank of Paris, and she was the furthest thing possible from a farmer's daughter.

I was thinking of this not long ago while skiing with my son and his two children. How happy I feel now, surrounded by wife and children and grandchildren—something I'd avoided throughout my life while chasing other men's daughters. Incidentally, the little turd Taki, just turned thirteen, is now so good a skier that the "race of the generations" has been permanently called off. He's just too fast and I'm just too old. So my son, his father, took pity and lied that the next race will take place some time in the future. The higher virtue of pity prevailed over the sin of pride. Yet I find great delight in that most basic and ordinary of occurrences: grandchildren schussing down mountains.

Taki is the oldest grandchild, and thinks of girls and football all day. Maria, eleven, thinks of what eleven-year-olds think all day, Antonius walks around showing off his tiny willy, and Theodora, the baby, sleeps.

Theodora is the prettiest little blue-eyed thing ever, even if I say so myself, but she did not wait and, yet again, I missed the birth. In fact, I've never been able to be there when it counts. I missed my daughter's birth, which she never forgets to remind me, because I was playing tennis in Palm Beach and got to New York ten minutes too late. I missed my boy's because I went to sleep and Alexandra chose not to wake me. My grandchildren Taki and Maria were born in Rome, and Antonius and Theodora in Salzburg. That makes it children and grandchildren: six; yours truly: zero.

Nothing to be proud of but I make up for it. After my father died I instructed the household to refer to me as the GP, for Great Provider. The children howled with laughter and mock anger, but the name stuck, and that's what the kids called me until they grew up. Then the Great Provider became the Great Pest. Now that I have turned everything over to them and the wife, I am the Great Pain. My daughter Lolly has three residences, my son JT has four, and poor little me is down to two, both in the name of the wife. What I need is a GP, as in a Great Psychoanalyst.

When the family gathers at my home in Gstaad, the wife no longer gives me hell after the occasional all-night bender, but now it is my daughter and son who refuse to tolerate any hanky-panky. And soon it will be the grandchildren. What fresh hell is this?

Not that there is much to do at night in Gstaad. The local beauties walk three abreast, giggle, and tell dirty old men who try to chat them up to fuck off. The only excitement recently was when my son-in-law discovered a book on the shelves written by yours truly thirty-five years ago, *Princes, Playboys, & High-Class Tarts*. He opened it and found a dedication from the author to the owner of the house we'd taken, who had been a great beauty. Apparently we tripped the light fantastic long ago and I put it on paper. No one in my family seemed to mind, but I did, having forgotten all about it.

If only they made a Viagra pill for memory loss. Indeed, at a splendid gathering in Paris given by Valentino, I'd been introduced to one of the most beautiful girls I've ever met. As we began to dance, I asked her name. She slapped me. It turned out we had lived together years ago.

All of which is to say that the following, in a nutshell, is what my life is like these days.

My wife and I decided recently to visit our daughter and son-in-law at their place in Austria. It is a full day's drive, so we set out early in the morning on a brilliant day, heading east. As I'd told my son, I can find Wolfsegg with my eyes closed and driving in reverse. But Alexandra was behind the wheel, and a terrible thing appeared: the GPS on her mobile, which she attached next to the steering wheel. It produced a pretentious-sounding English-accented female voice that started to boss us around. We were going toward Bern, then on to Zurich, Winterthur, Innsbruck, and so on, always heading east, so I told Alexandra to shut this bitch up and trust my vast experience. Nothing doing. As we approached Zurich, the voice became almost belligerent.

Turn here, turn there, go north, now southeast. We began to go around in circles.

I tried to convince the driver that I'm a great navigator, and that had I been born before Amerigo Vespucci, the U.S. would now be called Takiland. Back in the good old days, I told the wife, we went from point to point and never got lost. But to no avail. She followed the social climber's orders to the letter, so we continued to go around in circles. I insisted we were going in the wrong direction, but you know how women are, especially nowadays; they doubt men's opinions at all times.

Finally, I took the proverbial bull by the horns and turned the bloody machine off. But the end result was that instead of a pleasant seven- or eight-hour trip with stops at picturesque Austrian inns, it turned into a sixteen-hour marathon with poor Alexandra driving the whole way because I can't see after a certain hour. And there were no inns, and definitely no innkeepers' daughters.

By the time we arrived at my son-in-law's schloss, even I, who had done no driving, felt zombie-like. But I slept like a top, and woke up to a tiny, tiny baby asleep in her mother's arms, making funny noises that sounded almost like *papou*, the Greek word for grandfather.

ABOUT THE AUTHOR

Taki Theodoracopulos was the High Life columnist for London's *The Spectator* for more than forty years. He has written for *Esquire, National Review*, London's *Sunday Times*, the *New York Post*, and other publications. In addition to founding *The American Conservative* and *Taki's Magazine* (takimag.com), Taki is an avid sportsman who has played Davis Cup tennis, was a Greek karate champion, and won the gold once and bronze twice in the judo world championships' 70-and-over division.